WHAT THE BIBLE
SAYS ABOUT THE
SECOND
COMING

WHAT THE BIBLE
SAYS ABOUT THE
SECOND
COMING

Ralph Earle

BAKER BOOK HOUSE
Grand Rapids, Michigan

Contents

Contents

Preface

For over a century there has been an increasing interest in the subject of prophecy, and a whole library of books relating to it has appeared. In June, 1971, a great "Jerusalem Conference on Biblical Prophecy" was held in Israel. The return of Christ is a major theme of conversation and preaching among evangelical Christians.

At such times it is always necessary to set forth the basic truths in as simple and clear a manner as possible. That is what this book attempts to do.

The author makes no apology for the fact that his main approach is an attempt to see what the Bible says on the subject. To those who believe in the divine inspiration and authority of the Scriptures there is no other court of appeal. We have carefully and prayerfully sought to understand what God's Word teaches about the Second Coming and briefly to relate that to our times. We sincerely hope that this little volume will help people to be ready for the return of our Lord. Those of us who have experienced the salvation provided at the Cross, and who know the risen, living Lord in our lives, can only hope and pray that He will come back soon to complete His work of redemption.

The title of this book is found twice in the closing chapter of the Bible (Rev. 22:7, 12). It is the author's conviction that Jesus' promise, "Behold, I come," has fresh relevance for our day.

—RALPH EARLE

Introduction

What is meant by the word "prophecy"? The term "prophet" comes directly from the Greek *prophetes*. In classical Greek it was used for "one who speaks for a god and interprets his will."[1] In the New Testament the abstract noun *propheteia* means the "gift of expounding, or of speaking and preaching, under the influence of the Holy Spirit."[2] The verb *propheteuo*, "to prophesy," is used in the New Testament "in the primary sense of telling forth the Divine counsels . . . with the idea of foretelling future events (an idea merely incidental, not essential)."[3]

It is obvious that the main function of the prophet was that of forthtelling rather than foretelling. This becomes apparent to any thoughtful reader of the prophetic books of the Old Testament. The great eighth-century prophets—Isaiah, Hosea, Amos, and Micah—all have a relatively small element of *prediction* in their writings. The major thrust of their books is *preaching* against the sins of the people and calling wayward Israel back to God. The prophets were men who *spoke for God*, giving to His people the message of sin and salvation. And that is what true prophecy is.

The proper term to use for the study of future events is not "prophecy" but "eschatology." This term comes from the Greek adjective *eschatos*, meaning "last." So "eschatology" means "the doctrine of last things."

Another term that should be defined is "apocalypse." This is simply the Greek word *apocalypsis*, which means "an uncovering." In the New Testament it is translated "revelation." It properly refers to truth that is revealed by

9

God to man by inspiration of the Holy Spirit, and which could not otherwise be known.

Today the term "prophetic" is commonly used as a sort of combination of apocalyptic and eschatological. So we are almost compelled to use the word "prophecy" in this popular sense.

In his article on "Prophet, Prophecy" in *Baker's Dictionary of Theology*,[4] Andre Lamorte makes the following classification: "(1) Prophecies already fulfilled." These would include those concerning the exile of Israel and Judah, and the coming of Christ. "(2) Prophecies in process of fulfilment." He cites the setting up of the modern state of Israel in 1948. "(3) Prophecies not yet fulfilled." Of these he names four. "The first is the total recovery of Palestine by all the tribes of Israel. [But this has now taken place as the result of the famous Six-Day War of June, 1967.] The second is the destruction of Israel's enemies. . . . The third is the collective conversion of Israel. . . . The fourth is the establishment of the kingdom of God on earth."

In Chapter 1 we shall be looking at prophecies relating to the first coming of Christ. The ensuing chapters will be devoted primarily to what is foretold about the Second Coming. This will involve a study of what the New Testament has to say, from Matthew to Revelation. In connection with Revelation we shall have to look back to Daniel as the necessary background for understanding the Apocalypse. The final chapter will note the imminence of Christ's return in the light of current events.

1

In the Fullness of Time

Old Testament

Paul declares, "But when the fulness of the time was come, God sent forth his Son" (Gal. 4:4). For thousands of years people had waited longingly for this event. Jesus said, "Your father Abraham rejoiced to see my day: and he saw it, and was glad" (John 8:56). That was nearly 2000 B.C. But finally God's clock struck the appointed hour, and the long expected Messiah appeared.

Gen. 3:15 is often referred to as the Protevangelium ("first gospel") because it speaks of Christ as the Seed of the woman. In His death on the Cross, His "heel" (humanity) was bruised, but Satan's "head" (authority) was crushed.

Then the coming Messiah is presented as the Seed of Abraham. After that faithful patriarch had obediently placed his son on the altar, God said to him, "And in thy seed shall all the nations of the earth be blessed" (Gen. 22:18). Paul comments on this: "He saith not, And to seeds, as of many; but as of one, And to thy seed, which is Christ" (Gal. 3:16). Today all nations of the earth are being blessed with the salvation that Christ provided at Calvary.

In the third place, the Messiah would be the Seed of

David. That king was promised a "seed," which first meant Solomon. But then the prediction is extended far into the future: "And thine house and thy kingdom shall be established for ever before thee: thy throne shall be established for ever" (II Sam. 7:16). It was only in Christ that this promise was fulfilled. In the New Testament, He is frequently called "the son of David" (Matt. 1:1; 9:27; 15:22; 20:30; 22:42; etc.).

The coming Messiah is presented as *King* (I Chron. 17:12, 14; Ps. 2:6; 45:6; 110:1-2; Isa. 9:7; Jer. 30:9; etc.); as *Priest* (Ps. 110:4; Zech. 3:8); as *Prophet* (Deut. 18:15; cf. Acts 3:22; 7:37); as *Shepherd* (Isa. 40:11; Ezek. 37:24); and as *Judge* (Isa. 11:3; 16:5). He is the Servant of the Lord (Isa. 49:5-6; 52:13; 53:11). As such, He is the Suffering Servant (Isaiah 53), a truth which the Jews failed to grasp and so rejected Jesus as their Messiah. The suffering of Christ is described in vivid detail in Psalms 22, a passage which clearly portrays death by crucifixion. This is all the more remarkable, since the Jews did not practice crucifixion. How could the ancient Psalmist know that it would be Romans who would execute Jesus by their prescribed method of crucifixion? Clearly the Holy Spirit inspired this prophecy, which was literally fulfilled in Jesus' sacrificial death.

This is just a sampling of the many Messianic prophecies of the Old Testament. The fact we would emphasize is this: Since the predictions of Christ's first coming were all fulfilled, we have every reason to believe that the prophecies of His second coming will be fulfilled in their time. Logic and reason, alone, would demand this conclusion, and faith backs them up.

But now for a closer look at the phrase "in the fulness of time." There were three specific items that set the stage for the coming of Christ and the rapid spread of early Christianity.

The *first* was the *Roman government*, which united a

fragmented world. Here is the way J. Paterson-Smyth describes the earlier situation:

> A century before Messiah's day the world was intensely localized and subdivided and broken up into separate little nations, with their separate religions and customs and laws, their jealousies and suspicions, their constant wars, their bristling frontiers barring communication.[1]

But in the intervening hundred years the setting up of the Roman Empire changed conditions radically:

> When Jesus came, instead of frontiered nations separated and suspicious, He found a levelled world with the fences down. . . . The Roman roads traversed the civilized world, the iron power of the Caesars kept universal peace. The highway was open for the coming of the King.[2]

Never before nor since has the whole Mediterranean world been welded into one empire, under one ruling power. It was the perfect time for the universal Saviour to come.

A *second* factor was the *Greek language.* Not only could the early missionaries travel safely throughout the vast Roman Empire; they could preach in the same language everywhere they went. Again we say, such a situation has never existed before or since that day. If one were to try to preach the gospel in that same area now he would have to know Greek, Italian, Spanish, Slavic, Turkish, Hebrew, and Arabic. Paul preached in Greek from Damascus to Rome.

Not only that, but he had the sacred Scriptures in this one universal language. Between 250 and 150 B.C. the Hebrew Scriptures were translated into Greek. This version, called the Septuagint, was the Bible of the Early Church. It was the handbook of the first Christian missionaries.

It was Alexander the Great who spread the use of Greek from Europe to Asia and Africa in the fourth century B.C. Thus, in divine providence, the way was being prepared for the rapid spread of Christianity in the first century.

The *third* factor was the *Jewish religion.* Today Christianity dominates large areas of the globe. It is difficult for us to imagine the situation before Christ, when gross polytheism held sway almost everywhere.

But into that pagan world went the Jew with his monotheistic worship. It was a new message: "One God, lofty and holy, who valued righteous conduct, who cared for men, who listened to prayers, who intended some great thing in the future for humanity."[3]

The great Diaspora (dispersion) of the Jews began with the exiling of multiplied thousands of them in the eighth to sixth centuries B.C. With the Temple at Jerusalem destroyed by the Babylonians in 586 B.C., a new institution arose. It was the *synagogue*, or "gathering together," a term which first signified the congregation and then the place where the congregation worshiped. By the time of Christ there were Jewish synagogues in practically every major city of the Roman Empire. Wherever there were 10 adult male Jews in any community, it was their responsibility to establish a synagogue. James could say to the Jerusalem Conference: "For Moses from ancient generations has in every city those who preach him, since he is read in the synagogues every Sabbath" (Acts 15:21, NASB). The reading of the Mosaic law was heard in the synagogues each Sabbath not only by Jews but also by Gentile proselytes (converts to Judaism) and a still larger group of "devout men" who attended but did not join.

The Jews not only provided *monotheism* and the *synagogue*, but also a *Messianic hope*. In the century before Christ several Jewish apocalypses were in circulation. The most striking of these was the First Book of Enoch, which is supposed to have been written about 100 B.C. One passage in it reads:

> And in my vision I saw that with the Eternal was one whose countenance was like man and his face full of graciousness. And I asked the angel, and he said unto me, "This is the Son of Man, with whom dwelleth righteous-

ness and who reveals all that is hidden. . . . And this Son of Man will be a staff to the righteous and a light to the Gentiles and the hope of those who are troubled in heart. All who dwell on the earth shall bow the knee before him. For this reason he had been chosen before the foundation of the world and for evermore."

People's minds and hearts were thus being prepared for the coming of the Messiah. And come He did—"in the fulness of time." Just when the stage was set for him by the overruling providence of God, He stepped into history. And His coming marks the watershed of all history, for almost all nations date events B.C. (before Christ) or A.D. (in the year of our Lord). Therefore, whether it wishes to or not, the world bows at the manger every time a letter or document is dated, and subscribes to the fact that Jesus Christ is the supreme Lord of history. This glory belongs only to Him. Praise His name!

In his *Environment of Early Christianity*, S. Angus writes:

Christ appeared at the time when all the striving and hopes of all peoples were converging to a focus, when the vast majority of mankind were hungering for religious support, when East and West had been wedded, when men were expecting a new era, when the philosophy of Greece and the religious consciousness of the Hebrew were pointing toward a new Revelation.[4]

2

Watch . . . Be Ready

Synoptic Gospels

In studying a topic in the New Testament the logical place to begin is with the teachings of Jesus. Did Christ say anything about His return?

The answer is, "Yes." In Matt. 16:27, Jesus declares: "For the Son of man shall come in the glory of his Father with his angels; and then he shall reward every man according to his works." In the same context (Matt. 16:26 = Mark 8:36-37), it is typically reported with slight variation by another Synoptist: "Whosoever therefore shall be ashamed of me and of my words in this adulterous and sinful generation; of him also shall the Son of man be ashamed, when he cometh in the glory of his Father with the holy angels" (Mark 8:38). The third Synoptic Gospel records this important saying of Jesus in almost exactly the same form: "For whosoever shall be ashamed of me and of my words, of him shall the Son of man be ashamed, when he shall come in his own glory, and in his Father's, and of the holy angels" (Luke 9:26).

There is no way of applying these words to the first coming of Christ; they obviously refer to the Second Coming. The first time Christ came in humiliation and suffering, to die on the Cross for men's sins. The second time He will come in glory to rule over a redeemed creation.

Luke 18:8 contains another allusion by Jesus to His return: "Nevertheless when the Son of man cometh, shall he find faith on the earth?" This is line with Paul's statement that before the return of Christ in glory there will be an apostasy, a "falling away" from the faith (II Thess. 2:3).

In Luke 19:12-27 we find the parable of the pounds. This is not the same as the parable of the talents (Matt. 25:14-30). The former was spoken in Jericho, right after the conversion of Zacchaeus (Luke 19:9). The latter was spoken in Jerusalem, during Passion Week. Both point up the same lesson, but were delivered on different occasions and in different contexts.

In Luke 19:10 we find the key verse of that Gospel: "For the Son of man is come to seek and to save that which was lost." This expresses beautifully the purpose of Christ's first coming. He came to find the lost sinners of humanity and to save them. This is the distinctive emphasis of Luke's Gospel.

The purpose of the parable of the pounds is indicated in the eleventh verse: "And as they heard these things, he added and spoke a parable, because he was nigh to Jerusalem, and because they thought that the kingdom of God should immediately appear." The Jews expected the Messiah to come in glory and set up His kingdom in Jerusalem, ruling over the whole world. This was in line with many passages in the Old Testament (e.g., Psalms 24; Isaiah 11). What they did not realize was that the Messiah would first come to suffer and die for the sins of the world (Psalms 22; Isaiah 53). His coming in glory to reign over the world has not yet taken place. In the light of His crucifixion, resurrection, and ascension we can understand the distinction between His first and second coming as the Jews could not —not even the disciples before the Day of Pentecost (Acts

1:6). We now have the New Testament, plus the illumination of the Holy Spirit for understanding its truths.

In the parable of the pounds, Jesus told of a nobleman who "went into a far country to receive for himself a kingdom, and to return." This is exactly what He soon did, going away to heaven to receive the Kingdom from His Father. One day He will "return" to earth to set up here His kingdom of righteousness and peace—peace because of righteousness. The reason we do not have peace in the world today is that we do not have righteousness among men. Too often diplomacy is duplicity.

THE OLIVET DISCOURSE

This is the only long message of Jesus found in all three Synoptic Gospels (Matthew 24; Mark 13; Luke 21). And its subject is the Second Coming! This very significant fact should not be overlooked. It reveals a priority on the part of both Jesus and the Early Church.

It was perhaps Tuesday afternoon of Passion Week. As Jesus was leaving the Temple, His disciples came to Him and pointed out the magnitude and beauty of its buildings (Matt. 24:1). Josephus, the Jewish historian of the first century, says that the sanctuary was about 150 feet high. It was constructed of white marble, its roof gilded with gold. This was the magnificent temple that Herod had built shortly before the birth of Christ.

In answer to the eager excitement of the disciples Jesus said: "Verily I say unto you, There shall not be left here one stone upon another, that shall not be thrown down" (v. 2). These words were literally fulfilled in A.D. 70, when Jerusalem and its Temple were destroyed by the Romans. Josephus describes this event in almost the very words of Christ's prediction.

On their way back to Bethany, Jesus sat down on the western slope of the Mount of Olives, overlooking the

Temple area. The disciples came to Him privately and asked a threefold question: "Tell us, when shall these things be? and what shall be the sign of thy coming, and of the end of the world [literally, "age"]?" (v. 3) The Olivet Discourse, so called because it was given on the Mount of Olives, is the answer to these three questions.

The first question, "When will this happen?" referred to the destruction of the Temple, which took place in A.D. 70. This event is fully documented in secular history. In Rome one can stand before the Arch of Titus, near the Coliseum, and see engraved there the triumphal procession of this general (later emperor) who took Jerusalem. Some of the captive Jews are carrying the massive seven-branched lampstand ("candlestick") from the Temple.

In His reply Jesus dealt with the last question first (vv. 4-14). He said that many would come, claiming to be the Messiah (v. 5). One hundred years later Bar Cochba did make this claim. But he was taken by the Romans in A.D. 135 and Jerusalem was turned into a Gentile city, with no Jews allowed to live there. In modern times there have been a number of false messiahs.

Jesus went on to speak of "wars and rumours of wars" (v. 6), of famines and earthquakes (v. 7). Then He said, "All these are the beginning of sorrows" (v. 8). The last word is literally "birth pangs." These, together with persecution (v. 9), would be the birth pangs of the Messianic age. It is true that all of these things mentioned here have characterized every century of the Christian era. But they have been increasing in frequency and intensity as the end of the age has come nearer.

Christ sounded a warning that because of the prevalence of "iniquity" (literally, "lawlessness") the love of many would wax cold. This has taken place throughout Christendom in recent years. And when has there been more lawlessness in the supposedly civilized world than now?

The climactic sign of the end of this age is especially interesting. Jesus said: "And this gospel of the kingdom shall be preached in all the world for a witness unto all nations; and then shall the end come" (v. 14). Has this sign been fulfilled? It is true that not every *tribe* has heard the gospel. But it probably could be said that it has been preached in a measure to "all nations." It is our conviction that there is nothing in Christ's words here that would prevent His coming at any time.

The modern world missionary movement began with William Carey, in 1792. At about that time (1800) parts of the Bible had been printed in only 71 languages and dialects —50 in Europe, 13 in Asia, four in Africa, three in the Americas, and one in Oceania. But in the next 30 years 86 more languages received at least some of the Scriptures—more than in all the previous 1,800 years put together. In 1938 the number passed the 1,000 mark. Of these, 173 were in Europe, 212 in Asia, 345 in Africa, 89 in the Americas, and 189 in Oceania. The total figure has now gone well over 1,200 languages.

Another factor has entered the picture. Today there are hundreds of villages in Asia or Africa where no Christian missionary has ever gone, but where the people gather around a transistor radio to hear the message of salvation in their own language. The gospel is being preached to "all nations" as never before in the 1,900 years of Christian history. This is one of the many preparations for our Lord's return.

In the next paragraph (vv. 15-22) Jesus spoke of "the abomination of desolation"; that is, "the abomination that makes desolate," or desecrates the holy place. It is identified as having been "spoken of by Daniel the prophet" (cf. Dan. 9:27; 11:37; 12:11).

This apocalyptic expression is found elsewhere in the New Testament only in the parallel passage in Mark (13:14). For his Greek readers Luke (21:20) has substituted a much simpler wording: "Jerusalem compassed with armies." In reference to A.D. 70, then, the "abomination of desolation" would perhaps refer to the Roman eagle on the standards of the besieging soldiers. Also Josephus tells how the Zealots massacred their fellow Jews in the Temple during the siege of Jerusalem, thus desecrating the sacred place. In fact, "the abomination of desolation" may be translated, *the detestable thing causing the desolation* of the holy place."[1] Josephus felt that the destruction of the Temple was due to this act.

All of these interpretations refer to A.D. 70. Without doubt that is the primary application of Jesus' words, for Luke reports Him as saying: "When ye shall see Jerusalem compassed with armies, then know that the desolation thereof is nigh" (21:20).

What were the Christians to do? "Then let them which are in Judaea flee to the mountains" (Matt. 24:16; Mark 13:14; Luke 21:21). Eusebius in his *Ecclesiastical History* (A.D. 326) tells how this literally happened: "The whole body, however, of the church at Jerusalem, having been commanded by a divine revelation, given to men of approved piety there before the war, removed from the city and dwelt at a certain town beyond the Jordan, called Pella" (III, 5).

Luke finishes up this section on the destruction of Jerusalem in A.D. 70 by saying: "And they shall fall by the sword, and shall be led away captive into all nations: and Jerusalem shall be trodden down of the Gentiles, until the times of the Gentiles be fulfilled" (Luke 21:24). And that is exactly what happened.

The fourth paragraph of Matthew 24 (vv. 23-28) takes us back again to the signs of the Second Coming. We are told once more (cf. v. 5) that false christs and false prophets will appear, trying to "deceive the very elect" (v. 24). Then we have a graphic description of the suddenness of the Second Coming: "For as the lightning cometh out of the east, and shineth even unto the west; so shall also the coming of the Son of man be" (v. 27).

In the next paragraph (vv. 29-31) we are told that after the tribulation of those days there will be great portents in the sky: "And then shall appear the sign of the Son of man in heaven: and then shall all the tribes of the earth mourn, and they shall see the Son of man coming in the clouds of heaven with power and great glory. And he shall send his angels with a great sound of a trumpet, and they shall gather together his elect from the four winds, from one end of heaven to the other" (vv. 30-31; cf. Mark 13:26-27; Luke 22:27).

What "the sign of the Son of man" will be we do not know. It would be sheer speculation to hazard a guess. We simply note here Jesus' clear statement that "all the tribes of the earth . . . shall see the Son of man coming in the clouds." It will evidently be a spectacular appearance (v. 27) seen by all.

Again Luke gives a striking conclusion. He quotes Jesus' saying: "And when these things begin to come to pass, then look up, and lift up your heads; for your redemption draweth nigh" (Luke 21:28). There has never been a time since Jesus uttered these words that they have been more significant than right now! For "these things" are certainly beginning to come to pass.

Then Jesus gave the parable of the fig tree (vv. 32-35). The new life in the spring, putting out new leaves, is generally interpreted as referring to the revival of the nation of Israel. This application, which has been held for many years, has taken on fresh significance since the actual setting up of the state of Israel in 1948.

Christ concluded this parable by saying: "So likewise ye, when ye shall see all these things, know that it is near, even at the doors" (v. 33; Mark 13:29). "It is near" could equally well be translated "He is near"—in Greek the pronoun is included in the verb, with no indication of gender.

23

But since Luke's parallel passage (21:31) substitutes "the kingdom of God" for "it," probably "it" here should be taken as neuter.

Matt. 24:34 contains a very striking statement. But since we shall be discussing this at some length in the last chapter of the book, we pass it by for the present.

The last paragraph of Matthew 24 (vv. 36-51) stresses the suddenness of the Second Coming and our ignorance of when it will take place. Jesus said: "But of that day and hour knoweth no man, no, not the angels of heaven, but my Father only" (v. 36). After "angels of heaven" Mark adds: "neither the Son" (13:32). In the oldest Greek manuscripts the additional phrase occurs also in Matthew. So Jesus was saying that He himself, in His incarnation (cf. Phil. 2:5-8), did not know the time of His return. Certainly, then, we cannot know either.

Christ drew a parallel between the days of Noah and "the coming of the Son of man" (v. 37). In the time before the Flood people were "eating and drinking, marrying and giving in marriage" (v. 38). There is nothing wrong with any of these. But the point is that they were absorbed in physical satisfaction, neglecting their immortal spirits, and paying no attention to the preaching of Noah (II Pet. 2:5). They "knew not" (were unaware) until suddenly the Flood came and swept them all away. Jesus added, "So shall also the coming of the Son of man be" (v. 39). His coming will be sudden and unexpected.

What will happen then is spelled out precisely: "Then shall two be in the field; the one shall be taken, and the other left. Two women shall be grinding at the mill"—the little handmill in each home for grinding flour—"the one shall be taken, and the other left" (vv. 40-41). This highlights the fact that at the time of Christ's return there will be just two classes of people: those who are ready to meet Him and those who are not. The prepared ones will be "taken," the others "left." It will be a terrible time of separation of families and friends.

What is the keynote of the Olivet Discourse? Not the striking signs and spectacular portents that are described. The keynote is: Watch, and be ready! This note is sounded emphatically and repeatedly. It is the climax of this great message on the Second Coming. And that today should be the concluding emphasis of any sermon on this subject.

Jesus warned: "Watch therefore"—literally, "Stay wide awake!"—"for ye know not what hour your Lord doth come. Therefore be ye also ready: for in such an hour as ye think not the Son of man cometh" (vv. 42, 44). Again He said: "Watch therefore, for ye know neither the day nor the hour wherein the Son of man cometh" (25:13). Mark gives it just as emphatically: "Take ye heed, watch and pray: for ye know not when the time is. Watch ye therefore: for ye know not when the master of the house cometh, at even, or at midnight, or at the cockcrowing, or in the morning"—the four Roman military watches of the night—"lest coming suddenly he find you sleeping. And what I say unto you I say unto all, Watch" (13:33, 35-37). The closing word of the Olivet Discourse is "Watch"—"Keep awake!" or "Keep alert!" Luke concludes with this: "Watch ye therefore, and pray always, that ye may be accounted worthy to escape all these things that shall come to pass, and to stand before the Son of man" (21:36).

Matthew adds another chapter to the Olivet Discourse. Chapter 25 contains three parables—the 10 virgins, the talents, and the sheep and the goats. There are some who insist emphatically that the last of these is not a parable. But it is certainly put up in parabolic form, using sheep and goats as symbolizing two groups of people.

These three parables underscore three areas of preparation for the Second Coming. The parable of the 10 virgins (vv. 1-13) emphasizes the necessity of having our spiritual experience up-to-date and our hearts filled with the Holy

Spirit if we would be ready for Christ's return. The parable of the talents (vv. 14-30) calls attention to the importance of being good stewards of our time and money, of being busy at our Master's business, if we are to be prepared to meet Him. The story of the sheep and the goats shows that our treatment of our fellowmen, and especially those in need, will be a decisive factor in how we are judged by our Lord. All three of these phases are of supreme importance.

Let us look at each of these a little more closely. Jesus told of 10 virgins who took their lamps and went out to meet the bridegroom, who was coming to get his bride. The five foolish ones did not take an extra supply of oil; they did not provide for emergency. The "wise" (prudent) ones each took along an extra flask of olive oil.

The bridegroom was delayed, and finally the 10 virgins all went to sleep. Suddenly, at midnight, the cry rang out, "Behold, the bridegroom." The virgins all trimmed their wicks to make them shine more brightly. The wise ones re-filled their lamps. But the foolish begged: "Give us of your oil; for our lamps are gone out" (v. 8). The Greek says, "are going out." This is a sharp warning to us today. We may not be completely backslidden. But if our lamps are "going out," burning low, we should be concerned lest we not be ready when Christ comes.

In the Scriptures, both Old and New, oil is a type of the Holy Spirit. An important lesson of this parable is that we need to be filled with the Spirit if we are going to be ready to meet the Lord.

The climax of the parable comes in the words: "They that were ready went in . . . and the door was shut" (v. 10). The foolish virgins cried earnestly, "Lord, Lord, open to us." The tragic reply was, "I know you not." Those who were not ready were left outside in the darkness, while inside all was light, as the music and merriment of the wedding feast went on. It is a contrasting picture that should make every one of us pause and think, Am I ready? Right now?

There are some people who are strong on worship but weak on service. These need to heed the warning of the parable of the talents (vv. 14-30). It is not enough to take care of our spiritual devotion. We must be busy about our Master's business. We must use the talents He has given us in furthering the work of His kingdom.

A solemn warning is implied in this story. Too often the person who feels that he has only one talent decides there is no use trying and does nothing with it. To bury one's talent is to invite the Master's condemnation: "Wicked and slothful servant" (v. 26).

But there is a third area of preparation that Jesus called attention to. It is not enough to keep up our spiritual devotion and be busy in the Lord's service. We must also be kind and compassionate toward those in need. There are many evangelical Christians who give careful attention to worship and work, but they pay little attention to the distressing needs of the poor and underprivileged around them. They are so afraid of "the social gospel" and modern "social activism" that they shy away from any responsibility whatever in this area. But those who want to hear the Lord of all say at the Judgment Day, "Come, ye blessed of my Father" (v. 34), must merit the accolade: "Inasmuch as ye have done it unto one of the least of these my brethren, ye have done it unto me" (v. 40). Those to whom the Master says, "Inasmuch as ye did it not to one of the least of these, ye did it not to me" (v. 45), will hear Him voice these tragic words: "Depart from me, ye cursed, into everlasting fire, prepared for the devil and his angels" (v. 41).

We may feel that we can pass the tests presented in the first two parables. But how about the third? True Christianity is love. And true love is always outgoing, outflowing. The one who really loves is showing that love in kindly words and deeds to those in need.

Of Jesus it is said that He "went about doing good" (Acts 10:38). Is that said of us? If we want to be ready to

27

meet Him at His return, we must be His faithful followers. Are we following Him in this? If so, at the end of the road He will say, "Come in with Me." If not, He will say, "Depart from Me."

As He came to the close of His earthly ministry, Jesus was concerned that those who believed in Him would be ready for His return. He has told us how to be ready. We can't afford to fail in this the most important factor in life.

3

I Will Come Again

John

We have noted that the Olivet Discourse is the only long discourse of Jesus found in all three Synoptic Gospels. In the Fourth Gospel, John substitutes for this the so-called Last Discourse of Jesus (John 14—16).

The place is an upper room in Jerusalem. The time is the night before Christ's crucifixion. The scene is the Last Supper. Jesus was alone with His disciples just a few hours before His death. It was an epochal moment.

Judas Iscariot had left (John 13:30). Now the Master turned to His 11 apostles and said: "I'm going to be with you only a little while, and you can't go with Me when I leave" (vv. 33, 36). Looking at their troubled faces, Jesus began His discourse by saying: "Let not your heart be troubled: believe in God, believe also in Me" (14:1, NASB). He went on: "In My Father's house are many dwelling places; if it were not so, I would have told you; for I go to prepare a place for you. And if I go and prepare a place for you, I will come again, and receive you to Myself; that where I am, there you may be also" (vv. 2-3, NASB).

"I will come again"—this was Jesus' promise to His sorrowing disciples in the Upper Room. And it is still His message to us today. Regardless of how long He tarries, and how hard the way may become down here, the promise still stands. And it will be fulfilled in God's appointed time.

The main theme of the Last Discourse is the coming of the Holy Spirit as "the Comforter" (14:16, 26; 15:26; 16:7). This Greek word is *paracletos* (Paraclete), found only here and in I John 2:1, where Jesus is called our "advocate" with the Father. The word literally means "one called alongside to help." In John 14—16 it is most accurately translated "Helper" (NASB).

It is in the context of this teaching about the Holy Spirit that Jesus said: "I will not leave you comfortless"—Greek, "orphans"—"I will come to you" (14:18). This seems to have a different connotation from the promise, "I will come again," in verse 3. The addition there of "and receive you unto myself" seems clearly to indicate the Second Coming—Christ coming *for* His Church. But here (v. 18) it is Christ coming *to* His Church. What He is saying is this: "I will come to you in the person of the Holy Spirit"—at Pentecost. The context demands this.

Some years ago C. H. Dodd, the leading New Testament scholar in Britain, popularized the idea that whereas the Synoptic Gospels present a futuristic eschatology, the Fourth Gospel reflects a "realized eschatology." That is, Jesus' promises that He would return were fulfilled on the Day of Pentecost, when the Holy Spirit filled the hearts of the believers and made the presence of their risen, living Lord real to them.

Which is it? The answer is, "Both." Jesus did come to His disciples in a beautiful, satisfying way at Pentecost, so that they were not left as "orphans." The Master had promised that the Holy Spirit "will take what is mine and declare it to you" (16:15, RSV).

So the third and eighteenth verses of John 14 do not conflict with each other. Rather, they supplement one another. Jesus will come at the end of this age to receive His

Church to himself to be with Him forever. But meanwhile the Holy Spirit has come to make His presence real in our hearts and lives, and to "abide with you for ever" (14:16)— that is, with every believer everywhere, all the time. That is why Jesus could say: "It is expedient [profitable] for you that I go away: for if I go not away, the Comforter will not come unto you; but if I depart, I will send him unto you" (16:7). In His physical body Jesus was limited by space and time; He could be in only one place at a given moment. In the person of the Holy Spirit He would be with all His own all over the world at every instant. This is the glorious truth that the Lord wanted to impart to His disciples in the Last Discourse.

But John's Gospel does not teach only a realized eschatology—Jesus' presence with believers in this age. As we have seen, in 14:3 there is a clear promise of the Second Coming. But there is also another such promise at the close of the Gospel.

The twenty-first chapter is rather obviously an Epilogue to John's Gospel, as 1:1-18 is the Prologue. The purpose of this Epilogue is suggested in 21:20-23.

To get the occasion for this, we have to visualize the situation at about A.D. 95. John was the only one of the 12 apostles who was still alive. By that time, of course, he was an old man. He was probably about 25 years of age when Christ died in A.D. 30. That would make him about 90 years old when he wrote Revelation—and presumably his Gospel and Epistles. It was only natural that people would wonder if he was ever going to die!

That evidently became the basis for a rumor that Jesus had said John would not die (John 21:23). The Epilogue may have been written to squelch this false rumor. What Jesus had really said was, "If I will that he tarry till I come, what is that to thee?"

The phrase "till I come" (vv. 22-23) cannot refer to Pentecost, for it was written many years after that event.

The only logical reference it can have is to the Second Coming. So John's Gospel closes with the Church still looking for its Lord's return. This Gospel teaches both a realized eschatology and a futuristic eschatology.

4

This Same Jesus

Acts

The Book of Acts begins with the 40 days' post-resurrection ministry of Jesus, culminating in the Ascension (1:3-11). This climactic event became the occasion for one of the most definite promises of the Second Coming to be found in the New Testament. As the assembled disciples watched Jesus ascending bodily to heaven and disappearing in a cloud, two angels appeared and gave the glorious announcement: "This same Jesus, which is taken up from you into heaven, shall so come in like manner as ye have seen him go into heaven" (1:11). The *New American Standard Bible* reads: "will come in just the same way as you have watched Him go into heaven."

How did He go? Visibly, though seen apparently only by believers. When He comes for His Church, it will be just the same way. Lenski writes: "He departed visibly, he shall return visibly; he went to heaven, he shall come from heaven; he went away bodily, he shall come back bodily."[1]

There are those who would spiritualize all the references to Christ's return. They especially object to the phrase "the Second Coming." He has come millions of times, they say, to individuals all over the world. He is continually coming in forgiveness to sinners and in comfort to Christians.

All this is simply begging the question. It is true that He comes every day to all of us who love Him. But at the Ascension it was declared that He will "so come in like manner as ye have seen him go into heaven." At the end of this age there will be a visible, bodily return of our Lord.

The description also suggests that He will come unexpectedly. The disciples were talking with Jesus when suddenly, without warning, His body began to lift from the earth. In a number of places in the New Testament we are told that Christ's return will be sudden and unexpected (cf. Luke 12:39; I Thess. 5:2; Rev. 3:3).

Just as Jesus went in a cloud (v. 9), so He will come "in the clouds of heaven" (Matt. 24:30). Clouds are a symbol of grandeur, of the Divine Presence. It was a cloud that accompanied the people of Israel in the wilderness. When the Law was given to the Israelites at Sinai, a cloud covered the mount. It is fitting that Christ's ascension and second coming should be in the setting of clouds.

We know that Jesus was on earth nearly 2,000 years ago. We know that He ascended into heaven. With equal certainty we know that He will come again.

5

As a Thief in the Night

I and II Thessalonians

We now come to Paul's Epistles. The logical way to treat them is in their chronological order. Probably the majority of New Testament scholars would agree that the Thessalonian letters are the earliest of his extant Epistles. So that is where we begin. (Some hold to the priority of Galatians; but since that book contains no clear reference to the Second Coming, we bypass it here.)

I THESSALONIANS

I and II Thessalonians are the most eschatological of the Pauline Epistles. Again and again the apostle mentions the return of the Lord. He says of his readers: "Ye turned to God from idols to serve the living and true God; and to wait for his Son from heaven" (I Thess. 1:9-10). In 2:19 he speaks of "the presence of our Lord Jesus Christ at his coming." Again, he says: "And the Lord make you to increase and abound in love one toward another, and toward all men, even as we do toward you: to the end he may stablish your hearts unblameable in holiness before God, even our Father, at the coming of our Lord Jesus Christ with all his saints" (3:12-13). This is strikingly similar to 5:23—"And the very God of peace sanctify you wholly; and I pray God your whole spirit and soul and body be preserved blameless unto the coming of our Lord Jesus Christ." (Incidentally "at" in 3:13 and "unto" in 5:23 are the same in the Greek—*en*, which basically means "in.")

We should pause to note the close connection in these two passages between the holy life and the return of Christ. In fact, sanctification and the Second Coming are the two main emphases in I Thessalonians. And these are tied inevitably together. We need to be sanctified, filled with the Spirit, if we are to be ready for the coming of our Lord.

The outstanding passage in the New Testament on the rapture of the saints is I Thessalonians 4:13-18. It is well worth memorizing.

It would seem that when Paul founded the church at Thessalonica, he told his converts that someday Christ would return for His own. But in the meantime, some of the believers had passed away—were "asleep" in Jesus. The fear was that these might miss out on the Second Coming.

So Paul writes to assure the people. He says, "But I would not have you to be ignorant, brethren, concerning them which are asleep, that ye sorrow not, even as others which have no hope" (v. 13). Just as Jesus rose from the dead, "even so them also which sleep in Jesus will God bring with him" (v. 14). In fact, "We which are alive and remain unto the coming of the Lord shall not prevent"—rather, "precede"—"them which are asleep" (v. 15).

Then Paul goes on to describe what will actually happen: "For the Lord himself shall descend from heaven with a shout, with the voice of the archangel, and with the trump of God: and the dead in Christ shall rise first: then we which are alive and remain shall be caught up together with them in the clouds, to meet the Lord in the air: and so shall we ever be with the Lord" (vv. 16-17).

The apostle adds: "Wherefore comfort one another with these words" (v. 18). The "blessed hope" of the Second Coming is a very comforting truth to those who are ready to meet their Lord. At the same time it is a disquieting thought to those who are not ready. The Greek word for "comfort" can just as accurately be translated "exhort." All of us need to be exhorted to keep in constant readiness for the rapture.

Again (cf. Matt. 24:43-44) we are warned that Christ will come at a time when He is not expected: "For yourselves know perfectly that the day of the Lord so cometh as a thief in the night" (5:2). If people expected a burglar to break in, they would be watching for him. It is the unexpectedness of his coming that catches people unprepared. And so it will be with the coming of Christ. Since we do not know when He will appear, we need to be ready all the time.

But this warning is especially for sinners. For in the fourth verse the apostle writes: "But ye, brethren, are not in darkness, that that day should overtake you as a thief."

What will happen to the people of the world? The answer is graphic and disturbing: "For when they shall say, Peace and safety; then sudden destruction cometh upon them, as travail upon a woman with child; and they shall not escape" (5:3). The Second Coming will be a terrible time of disillusionment and distress for those who have ignored Christ's claims and instead have lived to please themselves.

II THESSALONIANS

In his Second Epistle to the Thessalonians, Paul makes this even more vivid. He speaks of the time "when the Lord shall be revealed from heaven with his mighty angels, in flaming fire taking vengeance on them that obey not the gospel of our Lord Jesus Christ: who will be punished with everlasting destruction from the presence of the Lord, and from the glory of his power; when he shall come to be glorified in his saints, and to be admired in all them that believe" (1:7-10). The first time Christ came in mercy to bring salvation. The second time He will come in judgment on the wicked.

In the second chapter of this Epistle, Paul deals with a different problem from that discussed in the fourth chapter of the First Epistle. There he had intimated that Christ might come at any moment. Twice he said, "We which are alive and remain" (4:15, 17). It sounds as though the apostle expected that he would still be living when Christ returned.

Apparently some of the Thessalonian Christians had gone to an extreme at this point. Perhaps it was some of these who had quit work. Instead of being busy, they were "busybodies" (3:11). Paul warns them to get back to work and earn their own living.

At any rate, we find a definite problem presented in 2:2. Paul writes: "That ye be not soon shaken in mind, or be troubled, neither by spirit, nor by word, nor by letter as from us, as that the day of Christ is at hand." The word "spirit" probably refers to a supposed revelation from the Holy Spirit, which apparently someone had voiced aloud in a church service. "Word" would be a reasoned message. The "letter" would be an epistle that was attributed to Paul. It is significant that this Epistle alone closes with an implied warning against forged letters. The apostle says: "The salutation of Paul with mine own hand, which is the token in every epistle: so I write" (3:17). What he rather obviously is saying is this: "Don't receive any letter as from me unless it is signed unmistakably in my own handwriting." It is shocking to think of anyone claiming Paul's authorship for letters he had not written. But such seems to have been the case.

From this "spirit," "word," or "letter" the Thessalonians had received the impression that "the day of the Lord is at hand." There is general agreement that the verb "is at hand" should be translated "has come" or "is already here." This was the heresy Paul was combating—the idea that Christ's return had already taken place.

Paul emphatically rejects this false notion and declares that the day of the Lord will not take place "except there come a falling away first, and that man of sin be revealed, the son of perdition" (v. 3). "A falling away" is in the Greek *he apostasia*, "the apostasy." In the best Greek text "man of sin" is "man of lawlessness." As early as the second century this phrase was identified with the "antichrist" of I John and "the beast" of Revelation. Today he is generally referred to as "the Antichrist."

He is described here as the one "who opposeth and exalteth himself above all that is called God, or that is worshipped; so that he as God sitteth in the temple of God, shewing himself that he is God" (v. 4). There seems to be a parallel here to the worship of the image of the beast (described in Rev. 13:11-15).

The expression "man of lawlessness" has become especially significant in the 1960's and '70's. Never was there a time when lawlessness was so rampant in civilized society. Never before have our policemen been called "pigs" and "law and order" been scoffed at by such a large segment of the population. Certainly "the mystery of iniquity"—Greek, "lawlessness"—"doth already work" (v. 7). How long will it be until "the man of lawlessness," the Antichrist, will be revealed? God alone knows the answer to that question.

Paul goes on: "Only he who now letteth will let, until he be taken out of the way." But "let" here means "hinder" or "restrain." Who or what is the restrainer? Commonly it is held that in Paul's day it meant the Roman Empire, which restrained lawlessness, but finally disappeared. Or it might mean the forces of law and order. With regard to the end of this age, it probably refers to the Holy Spirit, or the Church, or—to combine the two—the Holy Spirit in the Church. If we assume that the reign of the Antichrist and the period of the great tribulation will follow the rapture of the saints, this interpretation will harmonize with the words "until he be taken out of the way." Since the Holy Spirit was sent to indwell believers, it may be supposed that He will be taken up with the Church.

When this restraining Person or influence is removed, "then shall that Wicked be revealed" (v. 8). The Greek says, "Then shall the Lawless One be revealed." Obviously this is the same one who is called "the man of lawlessness" in verse 3 (a connection lost in KJV). This is the third time that "revealed" is used in this passage (cf. vv. 3, 6).

But this Lawless One is already doomed: "Whom the Lord shall consume with the spirit of his mouth, and shall destroy with the brightness of his coming." The word "spirit" should here be translated "breath." The Greek word *pneuma* primarily meant "breath" (cf. "pneumonia") or "wind" (cf. "pneumatic"), and then "spirit." What is stated here is that the Lord will destroy the Antichrist with merely "the breath of His mouth." What power!

"The brightness of his coming" is literally "the appearance of His coming." When Christ returns in power and glory, evil will be banished before Him.

This would be a good place to discuss the three Greek words used in the New Testament for the Second Coming. The one that occurs the least often (five times) is *epiphaneia*. Only here is it translated "brightness" (KJV). In the other four instances, all in the Pastoral Epistles (I Tim. 6:14; II Tim. 1:10; 4:1, 8; Titus 2:13), it is correctly rendered "appearance." When Christ returns, He will put in His appearance on earth again.

The next word is *apocalypsis*, from which we get "apocalypse." It simply means "revelation." It occurs 18 times in the New Testament and is translated six different ways in the King James Version—for example, "coming" (I Cor. 1:7), "appearing" (I Pet. 1:7). Twelve times it is translated "revelation," but in only one of these instances (I Pet. 1:13) does it refer to the Second Coming.

The most frequent term for the future coming of Christ is *parousia*. Literally it means "being beside," and so "presence." Six times it is used of a human being and two of these times it is translated "presence" (II Cor. 10:10; Phil. 2:12).

The other 22 times it is translated "coming." In 16 of these it refers to the Second Coming. Once it is used for the coming of the Antichrist (II Thess. 2:9). This is the great New Testament word for the second coming of our Lord—four times in Matthew 24 (3, 27, 37, 39), once in I Corinthians (15:23), four times in I Thessalonians (2:19; 3:13; 4:15; 5:23), twice in II Thessalonians (1:1, 8), twice in James (5:7, 8), three times in II Peter (1:16; 3:4, 12), and once in I John (2:28). To study these passages is to find the heart of the New Testament teaching on the Second Coming.

6

In the Twinkling of an Eye

Romans, I and II Corinthians

The Thessalonian letters were written from Corinth on Paul's second missionary journey about A.D. 50. The two Corinthian letters were written on the third journey, about A.D. 54 and 55. Romans was written about A.D. 56.

ROMANS

In the Roman Epistle, Paul was concerned primarily about the great doctrines of salvation—sin, justification, and sanctification. There seems to be in this long letter no clear, specific reference to the Second Coming. The nearest to it is probably found in 11:25-26—"Blindness in part is happened to Israel, until the fulness of the Gentiles be come in. And so all Israel shall be saved: as it is written, There shall come out of Sion the Deliverer, and shall turn away ungodliness from Jacob." A good case could be made for the assertion that "the fulness of the Gentiles" has been rapidly coming to a close with the setting up of the state of Israel in May of 1948 and the Jewish conquest of all Palestine in June of 1967. All this seems to point to the coming of the Deliverer, when "all Israel," as a nation, will be saved.

I CORINTHIANS

In I Corinthians much more is said about the return of Christ. In fact, it is introduced right away in the thanksgiving (1:4-9), which, as usual in Paul's Epistles, follows the opening salutation (vv. 1-2) and greeting (v. 3). The apostle writes to the Corinthians: "So that ye come behind in no gift; waiting for the coming [apocalypsis] of our Lord Jesus Christ: who shall also confirm you unto the end, that ye may be blameless in the day of our Lord Jesus Christ" (1:7-8). There is a sense in which He is now veiled to our eyes—"Whom having not seen, ye love" (I Pet. 1:8). His coming will be "the revelation" of Him, when we shall see Him face-to-face.

Again, Paul writes: "Therefore judge nothing before the time, until the Lord come, who both will bring to light the hidden things of darkness, and will make manifest the counsels of the hearts" (4:5). At present we do not have adequate basis for making fair judgments, because we do not know the motives of men. But all of this will become clear when Christ returns.

What is the main emphasis in the usual Communion service? Probably most people would agree that it is commemorating Christ's death for us on the Cross. So we sing songs about Calvary and the atoning Blood, and the whole service is marked by solemnity and a touch of sorrow.

Basically, of course, this is correct. But Paul points out the fact that there are three tenses in the celebration of the Lord's Supper (11:26). The first is the *past*—"Ye do shew the Lord's death." The second is the *present*—"As often as ye eat this bread, and drink this cup." The third is the *future*—"Till he come."

We should begin with meditation on the death of Christ for us. That should stir our hearts with sorrow and gratitude as we think of how He suffered in our place. But then we should feel a sense of joy in the reality of the presence of the risen, living Lord with us at the table. He died, but He is now alive, and we are having communion *with Him*.

We should not stop there, however. We are commemorating His death "till he come." That gives us a thrust upward and onward. If the thought of the Second Coming could be injected into every Communion, the participants would leave with a new joy and expectation. They would get a real "lift" out of the service.

In the second century, the Christians used to meet in private homes. In times of severe persecution they would gather in the early morning hours and disperse before daylight, so that they would not be caught and killed. Because they knew that each week might be their last on earth, they celebrated Communion every Sunday. And at the close of the service the whole congregation recited together the Aramaic expression *Marana tha* (I Cor. 16:22)—"Our Lord, come!" Perhaps our Communion services today would have new meaning if we would sing at the close some joyous song about the Second Coming.

I Corinthians 15 is the great Resurrection Chapter of the New Testament. Christ is the Firstfruits (v. 20), the first to have a genuine resurrection. (Others were raised from the dead, but died again.) And so we read: "But every man in his own order: Christ the firstfruits; afterward they that are Christ's at his coming *[parousia]*" (v. 23). The righteous will be resurrected at the time of the Second Coming.

The last seven verses of this chapter constitute another great passage on this subject, similar to I Thess. 4:13-18. It should also be memorized. Paul begins by saying: "Behold, I shew you a mystery; We shall not all sleep, but we shall all be changed" (v. 51). He goes on: "In a moment, in the twinkling of an eye, at the last trump: for the trumpet shall sound, and the dead shall be raised incorruptible, and we shall be changed" (v. 52).

These two verses, and especially the last clause, seem to indicate that Paul was expecting the Lord's return during his own lifetime: the dead will be raised, but "we shall be changed." Probably Paul clung to this hope until nearly the end of his life some 10 years later. This was natural in the light of the Ascension. If Paul was martyred about A.D. 65, this was only 35 years after the Crucifixion in A.D. 30. Probably most of the believers of that first generation expected the Parousia in their day.

The fact that they were personally disappointed in no way invalidates their Spirit-inspired teaching on the subject. Christ *will* return; that is an unassailable fact.

The coming of Christ will be sudden: "In a moment, in the twinkling of an eye." It will be loudly acclaimed: "The trumpet shall sound" (cf. I Thess. 4:16). As in that earlier Epistle, we are told that the dead (in Christ) will rise first. Then the living believers will be "changed" from mortal to immortal. The picture seems to be basically the same in these two passages, showing that the apostle had not changed his mind.

In the midst of the aches and pains, the troubles and trials of this life, we ought to turn to these great passages on the Second Coming and find renewed hope and courage. Though the battle may be long, our victory is assured. "But thanks be to God, which giveth us the victory through our Lord Jesus Christ" (v. 57).

7

Till the Day of Christ

Colossians, Ephesians, Philippians

The four Prison Epistles of Paul were probably written during the apostle's first Roman imprisonment (A.D. 59-61), in this order: Philemon, Colossians, Ephesians, Philippians. The Epistle to Philemon is really just a short personal note from Paul to his friend Philemon, asking him to take back his runaway slave, Onesimus. As would be expected, it has no direct doctrinal content and so no mention of the Second Coming. Therefore our study in this chapter will be confined to the other three letters.

COLOSSIANS

The one pertinent reference in Colossians is found in 3:4—"When Christ, who is our life, shall appear, then shall ye also appear with him in glory." The verb translated "appear" is *phaneroo*, related to *epiphaneia*, "appearance." In this world the followers of Christ are often despised. But at His return we shall appear with Him in glory to reign with Him forever.

EPHESIANS

In the Epistle to the Ephesians we find several indirect allusions to the Second Coming. Paul writes: "That in the dispensation of the fulness of times he might gather together in one all things in Christ" (1:10). This will take place at the time of Christ's return in glory (or at the end of the millennium).

Paul also declares that after his readers had believed (were converted) they were sealed with the Holy Spirit, who is "the earnest of our inheritance until the redemption of the purchased possession" (1:13-14). The Holy Spirit is the First Installment of our heavenly inheritance and the Divine Guarantee that we shall receive the rest—the word for "earnest" carries both ideas. The full possession of our inheritance will come when Christ returns to receive us to himself.

In view of this, we have the admonition: "And grieve not the holy Spirit of God, whereby ye are sealed unto the day of redemption" (4:30). If we want to redeem our inheritance when Christ comes back, we must keep the Holy Spirit ungrieved in our hearts. In modern Greek the word translated "earnest" (1:14) means an "engagement ring." The Holy Spirit is the Token Christ has given us of our betrothal to Him. If we retain that Token we shall be assured of a place at "the marriage supper of the Lamb" (Rev. 19:9), which will take place following the rapture of the Church.

This thought leads very naturally to the last allusion to the Second Coming in Ephesians: "Husbands, love your wives, even as Christ also loved the church, and gave himself for it; that he might sanctify and cleanse it [Greek, 'having cleansed it'] with the washing of water by the word, that he might present it to himself a glorious church, not having spot, or wrinkle, or any such thing; but that it should be holy and without blemish" (5:25-27). As suggested in the parable of the 10 virgins (Matt. 25:1-13), the return of Christ will actually be His coming to take His bride, the Church, to the eternal home He has prepared for her. This aspect of the Second Coming gives added beauty and romance to our expectation of the return of Jesus. We ought to look forward to that hour with something of the keen anticipation that a happy bride has in looking toward her wedding day. There is a sense in which we are "absent from the Lord" during this life (II Cor. 5:6). At the marriage supper of the Lamb we shall be united with Him forever.

PHILIPPIANS

The Prison Epistles are mainly Christological rather than eschatological. They deal largely with the richness of our life in Christ down here. But they do look forward to the culmination of this in the coming of the Lord to complete our redemption, as we find in the Epistle to the Philippians. It is reflected in the phrase "until the day of Jesus Christ" (1:6), or "till the day of Christ" (1:10). We live our lives here in the light of the Second Coming. That gives the needed incentive to holy living day by day, while we wait for our Lord.

In Phil. 3:20 we read: "For our conversation is in heaven; from whence also we look for the Saviour, the Lord Jesus Christ." The Greek word translated "conversation" is *politeuma* (cf. "politics"), which literally means "citizenship"—or, more exactly, "commonwealth." We do have citizenship down here, but we also have heavenly citizenship. We should live here as citizens of that heavenly realm, not as earthbound souls, with a low ceiling in life.

Philippi, to which Paul wrote this Epistle, was a Roman colony. Its citizens had the same rights as those who lived in Rome. But they also represented the Roman Empire. They were rich in both privilege and responsibility.

It is on the basis of this historical background that Moffatt translates this passage: "But we are a colony of heaven." It may also be rendered: "For our citizenship is in heaven" (NASB). As Martin Dibelius expressed it, "Our home is in heaven, and here on earth we are a colony of heavenly citizens." And so we should behave as such. To live as citizens of heaven—that is our high and holy calling.

At the Second Coming there will take place "the redemption of our body" (Rom. 8:23). Here Paul spells it out a bit more precisely. He says of Jesus: "Who shall change our vile body, that it may be fashioned like unto his glorious body, according to the working whereby he is able even to subdue all things unto himself" (v. 21).

The use of the word "vile" here is particularly unfortunate. The Greek does not suggest this at all. It simply says that Christ will change "the body of our humiliation" so that it will become like "the body of His glory." The translation "vile" reflects a Puritanic, if not actually Gnostic, distortion of New Testament teaching. These physical bodies of ours are not "vile." The Christian's body is the temple of the Holy Spirit (I Cor. 6:19). As such, it is holy. In itself there is nothing unclean or unholy about the human body. It is only the use that we make of it that will render it vile. A proper concept of the sanctity of the body is essential for wholesome living.

8

In the Last Days

I and II Timothy, Titus

Some scholars have pointed out the contrast between the emphatic eschatology of the Thessalonian and Corinthian letters and the paucity of this in the Prison Epistles. From this they have drawn the conclusion that, as Paul grew older and wiser, he became disillusioned with his earlier interest in the return of Christ. The Prison Epistles, they say, reflect his final shift to something of the "realized eschatology" attributed to John's Gospel.

The only way these scholars can hold such a view is to deny—as indeed they do—the genuineness of the Pastoral Epistles. For in the two letters to Timothy and the one to Titus we find a definite interest in the Second Coming.

I TIMOTHY

Paul writes to his younger colleague in the ministry: "Keep this commandment without spot, unrebukeable, until the appearing [epiphaneia] of our Lord Jesus Christ" (I Tim. 6:14). It is the imminent return of Christ that acts as a constant safeguard to us morally. If we knew that Christ was actually coming at this moment, we could not indulge in wrongdoing. A keen anticipation of the fact that He might come at *any* moment will keep us from sin.

In our childhood home a motto hung on the wall—one that is seldom seen today. It read:

> Do nothing you would not like to be doing when
>   Jesus comes.
> Say nothing you would not like to be saying when
>   Jesus comes.
> Go to no place where you would not like to be
>   found when Jesus comes.

That motto is even more relevant today as the moral standards around us are being lowered, and as the time of Christ's coming draws ever nearer. It could not only serve as a deterrent to worldliness, but it might help us to be more careful about saying unkind words or doing selfish deeds.

TITUS

The Epistle to Titus was written between I and II Timothy. It is here that we find the well-known phrase "that blessed hope." The passage reads: "Teaching us that, denying ungodliness and worldly lusts, we should live soberly, righteously, and godly, in this present world; looking for that blessed hope, and the glorious appearing of the great God and our Saviour Jesus Christ" (2:12-13). But the Greek says: "our great God and Saviour Jesus Christ"; that is, Jesus Christ is our God and Saviour—a clear affirmation of the deity of Jesus.

"That blessed hope" is "the glorious appearing" of Jesus, when He returns to earth. It is a hope that holds us steady in all the stress and strain of life. When things are depressing and discouraging, it gives us a lift. When things are dark and dismal, it gives us a light. When the outlook is dreary and distressing, it gives us a glorious uplook. Without this hope of the future, the present would sometimes seem unbearable.

II TIMOTHY

In the Second Epistle to Timothy the term "appearing" *(epiphaneia)* is used for both the first coming and the second coming of Christ. Paul speaks of a "holy calling," which was planned before the world began, "but is now made manifest by the appearing of our Saviour Jesus Christ, who hath abolished death, and hath brought life and immortality to light through the gospel" (II Tim. 1:10). This clearly refers to the first coming. But we also read: "Henceforth there is laid up for me a crown of righteousness, which the Lord, the righteous judge, shall give me at that day: and not to me only, but unto all them also that love his appearing" (4:8). Just as clearly this has reference to the Second Coming. It will be a time of rewards given to all those who have run the race successfully and reached the goal. It is called "that day" to distinguish it from all other days.

In II Tim. 3:1-5 we find a graphic description of "the last days." What does this phrase mean?

Probably in most people's minds the expression is taken as referring to the end of this age, the days preceding the Second Coming. But in Peter's speech on the Day of Pentecost we discover a wider meaning. Peter quoted Joel's prophecy, "And it shall come to pass in the last days, saith God, I will pour out of my Spirit upon all flesh" (Acts 2:17), and applied this to what happened on that day: "This is that" (v. 16). Clearly, then, "the last days" in their widest connotation mean "the days of the Messiah." They take in the whole period from Christ's first coming to His second coming. The Early Church was living "in the last days"—God's final day of dealing with mankind in and through His Son. (Compare Heb. 1:1-2 and Acts 2:17, where the phrase is used in the same way.)

But in II Tim. 3:1 we rather clearly have the expression "the last days" used for the closing days of this age, the time just before the return of Christ. Exactly the same usage occurs in II Pet. 3:3. It is common to find words and phrases used in the Bible in both a narrow sense and a wider sense. This is strikingly true of the phrase "in the last days."

The description of society at the end of this age (vv. 1-7)

bears striking resemblance to conditions as they have become in the last decade or two. Every word or phrase finds vivid application to the conditions in our own day. Men are "lovers of their own selves . . . disobedient to parents . . . without natural affection . . . lovers of pleasures more than lovers of God." Probably at no time in modern history has our society been characterized so generally by these attitudes as it is right now. These are surely "the last days."

Paul's "dying testimony" is given in II Tim. 4:7-8—"I have fought a good fight, I have finished my course, I have kept the faith: henceforth there is laid up for me a crown of righteousness, which the Lord, the righteous judge, shall give me at that day: and not to me only, but unto all them also that love his appearing."

The first clause is literally, "I have agonized the good agony." Our word "agony" comes from the Greek *agonia*, which was derived from *agon*, the word here translated "fight."

Agon, in turn, comes from the verb *ago*, which means "lead," and sometimes "lead together." So *agon* meant "a gathering." Since the largest gatherings in ancient Greece, as in modern America, were for sports events, the term *agon* came to be used especially for the gatherings for games— for instance, the Olympic Games—and then for the games themselves. And so the Greek verb *agonizo*, from which we get "agonize," meant to compete in an athletic contest. What Paul is saying here is, "I have competed well in the contest of life."

But since the main event of the Olympic Games was the marathon race (26 miles), he goes on to say, "I have finished my course." The word translated "course" comes from the verb meaning "to run," and so it signifies a racecourse. Following out this athletic figure, we might say that the third clause of verse 7 suggests: "I have kept the rules"—not "fouled out" or disqualified myself for the prize.

Because of this, at the end of the race Paul will receive

the "crown." The Greek has two words for crown: *diadema* (cf. "diadem") for a royal crown, and *stephanos* (used here), the laurel wreath given to the one who won the marathon race. This was the most coveted prize in ancient Greece.

Paul feels confident that he will finally break the tape at the winning line. There the "judge," the Umpire, will acclaim him the winner and give him the victory wreath.

But this will not be for him alone, but for "all them also that love his appearing." Everyone who is walking in the light, living close to God, and looking eagerly for the coming of Christ will receive the same crown. For in this race everybody who finishes successfully wins the prize.

9

The Day of the Lord Will Come

Hebrews and General Epistles

We noted earlier that some people object to the phrase "the Second Coming." They claim that Christ has come and is coming continually.

HEBREWS

To such objectors we would point out the use of the expression "the second time," in Heb. 9:28—"So Christ was once offered to bear the sins of many; and unto them that look for him shall he appear the second time without sin unto salvation." Christ came the first time to deal with the problem of sin. As the author says, "He appeared [in order] to put away sin by the sacrifice of himself" (v. 26). That was His purpose in coming to earth. In the preceding verses the writer of Hebrews draws a contrast between the repeated sacrifices of the Levitical priesthood—including the annual Day of Atonement (v. 7)—and the once-for-all sacrifice that Jesus made, in which He atoned for all the sins of all mankind everywhere.

But when He comes "the second time," it will be "without sin"—literally, "apart from sin." At His first coming Christ dealt effectively and finally with this problem. He will not have to face again the matter of "sin"—which can be interpreted as meaning "a sin offering." He has already made a full atonement.

The second time He will come "unto salvation." All that His death on the Cross provided will finally be realized at the time of His return. We shall have not only redeemed spirits, as now, but redeemed bodies (Rom. 8:23). In fact, all creation will share in this final "salvation"—"Creation itself will also be freed from the slavery of corruption into the glorious freedom of the children of God" (Rom. 8:21, literal translation). What a prospect! No more curse on creation, which came as a result of man's sin. This will be final salvation.

JAMES

The Epistle of James deals mostly with matters of practical ethics for life in this world. But there is one brief eschatological passage (5:7-8). James writes: "Be patient therefore, brethren, unto the coming of the Lord. . . . Be ye also patient; stablish your hearts: for the coming of the Lord draweth nigh." We must live each day in the light of the final day, when our Lord will return. It sometimes seems down here that evil is rewarded with fame and fortune, while good goes unnoticed. But all the wrongs of this life will be righted in the next. We can afford to wait for Christ to come back and set up His righteous rule over the world.

I PETER

And so we read in I Pet. 5:4 that "when the chief Shepherd shall appear, ye shall receive a crown of glory that fadeth not away." The crown was the *stephanos*, the laurel wreath (see discussion of II Tim. 4:8) that faded. But this one "fadeth not away" forever.

There is a beautiful trilogy of psalms, the significance of which is too often missed. In Psalms 22, with its vivid portrayal of the sufferings of crucifixion, we see the *Good*

Shepherd, who gives His life for the sheep (John 10:11). In Psalms 23, with its delightful picture of green pastures and quiet waters, we see the *Great Shepherd* (Heb. 13:20), who constantly cares for His own. In Psalms 24, with its "Lift up your heads, O ye gates . . . and the King of glory shall come in," we see the *Chief Shepherd,* who will come with royal splendor. He came the first time in humiliation to die on the Cross. He will come the second time in glory to rule the world.

If we accept Christ not only as our Saviour but also our Shepherd, with all that this implies, we shall be ready someday to rule with Him. ("Shepherd" also means "ruler.")

II PETER

The third chapter of II Peter is one of the greatest passages on the Second Coming to be found in the New Testament. We begin with verses 3 and 4: "Knowing this first, that there shall come in the last days scoffers, walking after their own lusts, and saying, Where is the promise of his coming? for since the fathers fell asleep, all things continue as they were from the beginning of the creation."

The last statement is manifestly absurd. But that's what Peter tells us the skeptics of the last days will say.

And they are saying it. We are informed frequently that history repeats itself, that it moves in cycles. And of course this is partially true. But there have been great *cataclysms* and *catastrophes*—two good Greek words—that have largely changed the course of history. The map of Europe, for instance, has never been the same since Napoleon lived or since Hitler died.

"All things continue as they were from the beginning of creation"? Everything that is happening has happened? When before 1945 did man harness the power of the atom, or before 1959 set a satellite in orbit around the earth, or before 1969 walk on the moon? To name a few of only the more recent developments. Nothing new under the sun? Peter says that these scoffers are "willingly ignorant" (v. 5).

Someone has said:

> In a sense, all previous historical crises were of the same kind, on the same level. What is not often appreciated is the radical, qualitative newness of recent developments. They are different in kind from anything that has gone before and fulfill the ancient prophecies in new, unprecedented ways.

In verses 6 and 7 we are reminded that the population of the earth was once largely destroyed by the Flood but that the next time it will be destroyed by fire. Water proved to be inadequate as a cleansing agency; fire will be more effective.

Sometimes it seems a very long time since Jesus was on earth. But we are informed that "one day is with the Lord as a thousand years, and a thousand years as one day" (v. 8). So in God's sight only a couple of days has passed since Christ came to earth. The reason that God postpones the inevitable day of judgment is that He is "not willing that any should perish, but that all should come to repentance" (v. 9).

Then a sharp warning is sounded: "But the day of the Lord will come as a thief" (v. 10). It has tarried long. But when the appointed time arrives, it *will* come as unexpectedly as a thief at night.

The description of what will happen is very vivid: "In the which the heavens shall pass away with a great noise, and the elements shall melt with fervent heat, the earth also and the works that are therein shall be burned up."

These words of Peter, written 1,900 years ago, are usually dismissed as the poetic extravaganza of an overheated imagination or at best interpreted as figurative, apocalyptic vocabulary. But in this atomic age we realize that the language used here could be fulfilled with terrible literalness.

When the first atomic bomb was experimentally exploded over the white sands of New Mexico, it blasted out a crater big enough to hold half a dozen houses. At the bottom of the hole the sand was fused into molten glass. It is claimed that at the moment of detonation of a nuclear weapon, heat is generated equal to that at the center of the sun. The only two atom bombs ever used in war killed about 100,000 people. Many years ago we read in the newspaper a statement made by a naval official in Washington. He said: "We now have in our possession one bomb that if dropped over Manhattan would destroy 14 million lives." That is the kind of world we live in today.

Peter, like Paul, is always concerned about the practical application to Christian living. So he continues: "Seeing then that all these things shall be dissolved, what manner of persons ought ye to be in all holy conversation and godliness, looking for and hasting unto the coming of the day of God, wherein the heavens being on fire shall be dissolved, and the elements shall melt with fervent heat" (vv. 11-12).

The term "conversation" here means "manner of living." There are three Greek words in the New Testament that are translated "conversation" (in KJV), none of which means what we understand by that term today. If the modern reader will cross out "conversation" and write "conduct" in its place he will have the correct translation. (That's what "conversation" meant in 1611.)

It is generally agreed that the expression "hasting unto the coming" should be translated "hastening the coming." How can we hasten Christ's return? For one thing, He told us to pray, "Thy kingdom come." Perhaps our prayers could hasten that event, not only spiritually during this age but fully at the Second Coming. Then, too, Jesus said: "This gospel of the kingdom shall be preached in all the world for a witness unto all nations; and then shall the end come" (Matt. 24:14). One way we can hasten the Lord's return is by finishing the task of evangelizing the world. The job could be completed in our generation if we had more men like William Carey, who was largely responsible for translating the Scriptures in whole or in part into 40 different languages. While most of us will never go to foreign shores as missionaries, we can all give and pray to hasten the day.

The blessed hope looks beyond the judgments that will come on the world at Christ's return in glory and sees "new heavens and a new earth" (v. 13). This subject is developed at length in the last two chapters of Revelation. So we leave its discussion to that point.

Again Peter makes the application: "Wherefore, beloved, seeing that ye look for such things, be diligent that ye may be found of him in peace, without spot, and blameless" (v. 14). This should be our constant concern if we are to be ready to meet Jesus when He comes again.

I John

The First Epistle of John is concerned primarily with the believer's walk in this world. But as with Paul, this is related to the Second Coming. For instance, John says: "And now, little children, abide in him; that, when he shall appear, we may have confidence, and not be ashamed before him at his coming" (2:28).

In the third chapter John goes on to say: "Beloved, now are we the sons of God, and it doth not yet appear what we shall be: but we know that, when he shall appear, we shall be like him; for we shall see him as he is. And every man that hath this hope in him purifieth himself, even as he is pure" (vv. 2-3). The blessed hope is a purifying hope.

There are some people who take the attitude that, since we are going to be made like Jesus when we meet Him, there is no need to seek to be like Him now. But that is selfish. If we really love Him we will long to be like Him. We will seek to purify ourselves from all unchristlike attitudes, words, and actions. We will ask the Holy Spirit to make us more like our Lord, so that we shall not be ashamed to meet Him when He comes for His bride.

10

Surely I Come Quickly

Revelation

The key to understanding the Book of Revelation is suggested in the first verse. It is a revelation from God through Jesus Christ to John. It was given to show His servants "things which must shortly come to pass . . . sent and signified . . . by his angel unto his servant John."

There are three words here that require special comment. The first is *must*. These things *must* come to pass because God has decreed that they shall. Here is a strong emphasis on divine sovereignty. We need not wonder how everything will finally come out, for a sovereign God is in control; the fulfillment of His purposes is absolutely certain.

The second word is *shortly*. This underscores the idea of imminence. These things will happen soon. Yet the term must be interpreted from God's point of view, not ours. As we have already noted, a thousand years is only one day with Him. So there is no conflict between the "shortly" and the fact that nearly 1,900 years have gone by. William Newell makes this helpful comment: "'Shortly,' moreover, not only means imminency, but also *rapidity of execution* where action once begins."[1] We believe that this twofold application is correct.

The third word is *signified*. The Greek verb literally means "to show by a sign." McDowell writes: "The author implies that the message he has received is being given to his readers under signs or symbols. Attention to this fact should save us from crass literalism in interpreting the message of the book."[2] It would help if we pronounced the word as *sign-i-fied* and interpreted the book symbolically, as it was clearly intended to be taken.

There are three main schools of interpretation of Revelation. The *preterist* view holds that all the events pictured here took place in the period of the Roman Empire. The *historicist* view maintains that these events have been taking place all through the Church age. The *futurist* view holds that everything beginning with chapter 4 is yet to be fulfilled.

The first clear reference to the Second Coming is in 1:7—"Behold, he cometh with clouds; and every eye shall see him, and they also which pierced him: and all kindreds of the earth shall wail because of him. Even so, Amen." This verse is based largely on Dan. 7:13 and Zech. 12:10, but probably more immediately on Matt. 24:30, where Christ makes the same combination. Besides these two passages, the coming with clouds is mentioned in the New Testament in five other places (Matt. 26:64; Mark 13:26; 14:62; Luke 12:27; Rev. 14:14). Those who have rejected Christ will see Him when He returns in glory, and they will "wail" as they realize how they have spurned His love and rejected His salvation.

Some eight chapters of the book are taken up with a highly symbolical description of three series of judgments: the Seven Seals (cc. 6—7), the Seven Trumpets (cc. 8—11), and the Seven Bowls (cc. 15—16). In between the last two we find a Sevenfold Vision (cc. 12—14). Futurists generally interpret this as taking place during the so-called great tribulation. The name comes from 7:14, which literally reads: "These are the ones who come out of the great tribulation."

It is extremely difficult to place the events of this central section of Revelation in chronological order. Probably the three series of judgments noted above should be treated as concentric rather than successive.

This is suggested by the fact that the seventh seal becomes the seven trumpets (8:1-2) and that the seventh trumpet takes us to the final culmination: "And the seventh angel sounded [on his trumpet]; and there were great voices in heaven, saying, The kingdoms of this world are become the kingdoms of our Lord, and of his Christ; and he shall reign for ever and ever" (11:15; cf. 1:7). So the seven bowls which follow (cc. 15—16) would seem to cover the same period of time. They are described as "the seven last plagues; for in them is filled up the wrath of God" (15:1). This will be the time of God's final judgment on the earth.

THE GREAT TRIBULATION

This name is usually given to a specific period of three and a half years at the end of this age. The length of time is based on three expressions that occur several times in the Book of Revelation. The first is "forty-two months" (11:2), which is obviously the same as the 1,260 days of verse 3. The first of these two notations of time occurs again in 13:5 —"And there was given unto him [the beast, commonly known as the Antichrist] a mouth speaking great things and blasphemies; and power was given unto him to continue forty and two months." The second notation is found again in 12:6—"a thousand two hundred and threescore days." The same length of time is expressed in still a third way: "a time, and times, and half a time" (12:14).

It is obvious that all three expressions mean the same thing: three and a half years. To what does this apply?

There are two significant historical references. The first is that of the severe persecution of the Jews by Antiochus Epiphanes (168-165 B.C.). The second is the time of the Jewish revolt against Rome (A.D. 66-70). During this period the

Jewish Christians in Jerusalem fled to Pella, where they escaped the horrible sufferings of those who remained in that besieged city. If the Book of Revelation was written during the persecution of the Christians by the Emperor Domitian (A.D. 95), as seems most likely, then both these historical events were in the past. So it is common today to apply these time references to the great tribulation at the end of this age, when the Antichrist will persecute both Jews and Christians.

SEVENTY WEEKS

The Book of Revelation can be understood only in the light of its background in the Book of Daniel. In fact, Revelation contains some 70 allusions to Daniel. So if we want to know the origin of the idea of three and a half years we must turn back to that Old Testament book.

In the prophecy of Jeremiah (23:12; 29:10), Daniel discovered the prediction that the Lord "would accomplish seventy years in the desolations of Jerusalem" (Dan. 9:2). The period of the Babylonian captivity as specified by Jeremiah was from about 606 B.C., when Daniel was taken captive, to 536 B.C., when the Jews under Cyrus began returning to Jerusalem.

Noting that the 70 years were up, Daniel gave himself to fasting and prayer, confessing the sins of his people and petitioning for forgiveness (9:19). In answer to his praying, the angel Gabriel appeared and gave him this special message: "Seventy weeks are determined upon thy people and upon thy holy city, to finish the transgression and to make an end of sins, and to make reconciliation for iniquity, and to bring in everlasting righteousness, and to seal up the vision and prophecy, and to anoint the most Holy" (9:24). The last part of this seems definitely to look forward to the second coming of Christ.

Gabriel continued: "Know therefore and understand, that from the going forth of the commandment to restore and to build Jerusalem unto the Messiah the Prince shall be seven weeks, and threescore and two weeks. . . . And after threescore and two weeks shall Messiah be cut off, but not for himself" (9:25-26). This makes 69 weeks before the death of the Messiah.

What is the starting date for these 69 weeks? It is often assumed that the reference in verse 25 is to the decree of Cyrus for the return of the Jews to Palestine (II Chron. 36: 32; Ezra 1:2-4). That decree was made in 538 B.C. If this is the "commandment" referred to in Daniel, then the prediction "missed it" by about a century.

But a careful reading of both records of this decree of Cyrus shows that nothing was said about restoring or building Jerusalem (Dan. 9:25). Cyrus said that the Lord of heaven had commanded him to "build him an house in Jerusalem." So he told the Jews to "go up to Jerusalem, which is in Judah, and build the house of the Lord God of Israel" (Ezra 1:3).

When was the commandment made to restore and rebuild Jerusalem? The answer is: In 444 B.C., when Nehemiah was commissioned by King Artaxerxes to go to Jerusalem and rebuild its walls and houses (Neh. 2:1-9).

Everyone is agreed that in apocalyptic language a "week" means seven years. This is what is called the "day= year" principle of prophecy. Multiplying 69 by 7 we come up with 483 years. But the calendar of that time was based on the lunar year of 360 days. So the 483 solar years would equal 471 lunar years. Christ (the Messiah) was "cut off" (crucified) in A.D. 30. If we subtract this 30 from 471 it gives 441 B.C., which is very close to 444. In other words, Daniel predicted the time of Christ's crucifixion to within three years. This is an equally supernatural miracle, whether we follow the conservative date for the writing of Daniel in the sixth century B.C. or the liberal date in the second century B.C.

But we are particularly interested in the seventieth

week. We read in Dan. 9:27—"And he shall confirm the covenant with many for one week: and in the midst of the week he shall cause the sacrifice and the oblation to cease, and for the overspreading of abominations he shall make it desolate, even until the consummation, and that determined shall be poured upon the desolate."

The first and most obvious application of this would be to Antiochus Epiphanes, the Seleucid king of Syria who persecuted the Jews severely for three and a half years (168-165 B.C.), desecrating their Temple and seeking to destroy their religion. Finally the Maccabean forces recovered Jerusalem in 165 B.C., and cleansed and rededicated the Temple. This was celebrated in Jesus' day by the Feast of Dedication (John 10:22). Today the Jews still observe it in what they call Hannukah, or the Feast of Lights, held in December every year.

We have already noted that in the Book of Revelation there are several references to a period of three and a half years. Bible students have commonly identified this with the second half of Daniel's seventieth week and designated it "the great tribulation"—the time when the Antichrist will oppress God's people.

It is obvious that if this interpretation is adopted the Church age must be inserted between the sixty-ninth and seventieth weeks. And there is a break at that point in Daniel. Moreover, the account says, "Seventy weeks are determined upon thy people and upon thy holy city" (Dan. 9:24). It is evident, then, that the 70 weeks relate to the history of the Jews in Jerusalem. That was practically set aside from the first century to the mid-twentieth century. So it seems entirely logical to identify the seventieth week with a period at the end of this age.

Sometimes it has been assumed that the great tribulation will last for seven years. But both Dan. 9:27 and the references in Revelation point to a three-and-one-half-year period of actual persecution.

68

THE ANTICHRIST

In the second century Irenaeus identified both "the man of lawlessness" of II Thessalonians (2:3) and "the beast" of Revelation (19:20) as the Antichrist. Though the word "antichrist" occurs only in I John (2:18, 22; 4:3) and II John (7), it seems wise to adopt this identification which has commonly been made for 1,800 years.

The beast is described in the thirteenth chapter of Revelation. In fact, there are two beasts—one out of the sea (13:1-10) and one out of the earth (13:11-18). But it is the first that is later called "the beast." The second is referred to as "the false prophet." The first represents civil power, the second religious power.

The description in verse 1 refers first of all to the Roman Empire, on whose "heads" (emperors) were the names of blasphemy. Nero called himself "Saviour of the World." Domitian, the current emperor, was called "Our Lord and our God." The Antichrist will likewise claim to be Deity. It is said of him that "he opened his mouth in blasphemy against God, to blaspheme his name" (v. 6). He will "make war with the saints" (v. 7)—God's people, both Jews and Gentiles. Authority will be given him "over all kindreds, and tongues, and nations." Probably the Antichrist will be the first man ever to rule the whole world.

This might be the place to make an observation. Never before in all the history of humanity has it been actually possible for one man to rule over the entire globe. But now with worldwide, live television by means of space satellites over the oceans, a man can be seen and heard simultaneously around the earth. Furthermore, intercontinental ballistic missiles could quickly destroy any city or country that defied the orders issued over television. The stage is set as never before for the appearance of the Antichrist, and also for the coming of Christ—"and every eye shall see him" (1:7). This could not be true until the present decade.

We are also told that "all that dwell upon the earth shall worship" the Antichrist—those "whose names are not written in the book of life of the Lamb slain from the foundation of the world" (13:8). Today worldwide simultaneous worship via live television is a practical possibility. Even now millions of people across America share at the same moment in televised worship services.

The last three verses of chapter 13 have occasioned a great deal of speculation. We read that all people will have to "receive a mark in their right hand, or in their foreheads: and that no man might buy or sell, save he that had the mark, or [better, 'that is'] the name of the beast, or the number of his name" (vv. 16-17). It would be idle to speculate just what form this will take. Some claim that the use of one's social security number, plus the central computer storage of personal data on all citizens of the United States, is an indicator of this fulfillment, but this is a worldwide prophecy, not just one for the United States.

What does the number 666 represent? The field has been wide open on this point. Very probably it did originally represent Nero.[3] In modern times the number has at various times been identified with Kaiser Wilhelm, Mussolini, and Hitler. All these speculations proved to be wrong, and we should heed the warning against all such idle theorizing.

What we need to do is to note what the Scripture itself says: "It is the number of a man." Throughout the Bible seven is a symbolic number of perfection. So the number six represents man as less than perfect. "The number 666 simply multiplies threefold this idea that man is imperfect." The worship of the beast, whose number is 666, underscores a fact that is increasingly plain: "This age will end with the worship of man, instead of the worship of God."[4] The "Death of God" theology was one recent manifestation of this, and another is the growing influence of atheistic Communism.

ARMAGEDDON

The Antichrist is connected in most people's minds with the Battle of *Armageddon*. This word is found only once in the New Testament, in Rev. 16:16. In order to unstand it we need to look at the context.

In connection with the "sixth bowl" we read: "And I saw three unclean spirits like frogs come out of the mouth of the dragon, and out of the mouth of the beast, and out of the mouth of the false prophet" (v. 13). Here we see the trinity of evil, opposing the Holy Trinity. "The dragon" is a symbolical name for the devil, or Satan (20:2). "The beast" is the first beast of chapter 13, the Antichrist. "The false prophet" is the second beast of chapter 13, the one who caused people to worship the first beast. Out of the mouths of these three come "three unclean spirits," who are "the spirits of devils [demons], working miracles, which go forth unto the kings . . . of the whole world, to gather them to the battle of that great day of God Almighty" (v. 14).

Verse 15 is an interlude of warning from Jesus: "Behold, I come as a thief." This is the third time we have found this phrase "as a thief" in connection with the Second Coming (cf. I Thess. 5:2; II Pet. 3:10). Then the Lord adds: "Blessed is he that watcheth"—that is, "keeps awake" (cf. Matt. 24:42; 25:13).

In verse 16 the "battle of that great day" is identified as the Battle of Armageddon. We read: "And he [rather, 'they,' the three unclean spirits] gathered them [the kings of the whole world (v. 14)] together into a place called in the Hebrew tongue Armageddon." This word is generally interpreted as meaning "the Mount of Megiddo," which is a hill on the south side of the long plain (Esdraelon) that separates Galilee in the north from Samaria to the south. It was here that Sisera and his host were defeated (Judg. 5:19). Here also the death of Ahaziah, king of Judah, took place (II Kings 9:27). The saddest incident was the killing here of good King

Josiah by Pharaoh-nechoh of Egypt (II Kings 23:29). Ewing writes:

> These low hills around Megiddo, with their outlook over the plain of Esdraelon, have witnessed perhaps a greater number of bloody encounters than have ever stained a like area of the world's surface. There was, therefore, a peculiar appropriateness in the choice of this as the arena of the last mighty struggle between the powers of good and evil.[5]

On this brief reference in 16:16 to Armageddon, George E. Ladd comments: "This is preparatory for the actual battle which takes place in 19:11 ff. when Christ comes as a victorious warrior to defeat his foes."[6]

Chapters 17 and 18 describe the fall of Babylon, which is pictured as a prostitute decked out in purple and scarlet and riding on a scarlet beast (17:3-4). On her forehead, like Roman prostitutes of that day, she carried her name (17:5). The first word, MYSTERY, alerts us to the fact that the name is to be taken as symbolical.

What is meant by Babylon? Without doubt, for the readers of the first century it meant Rome, which ruled the world of that day. As for us, the symbol probably stands for the government of the Antichrist, the world ruler who will appear at the end of this age.

The beast had 10 horns. These are identified in 17:12—"And the ten horns which thou sawest are ten kings which have received no kingdom as yet; but receive power as kings one hour with the beast." This is generally interpreted as referring to a confederation of 10 rulers at the end of this age, under the control of the Antichrist. The nearest kind of this we have today is the increasing number of satellite countries dominated by Communism. But it would be idle to try to identify the 10.

The account goes on to say: "These shall make war with the Lamb, and the Lamb shall overcome them: for he is

Lord of lords, and King of kings" (v. 14). This will take place at the Battle of Armageddon.

It would appear that this battle is described at more length in 19:11-21. Christ—who is described as "Faithful and True" (v. 11) and "The Word of God" (v. 13)—comes out of heaven riding on a white horse, with the armies of heaven following Him. He is also called KING OF KINGS, AND LORD OF LORDS (v. 16).

Then John "saw the beast, and the kings of the earth, and their armies, gathered together to make war against him that sat on the horse, and against his army" (v. 19). It is generally held that this is the Battle of Armageddon, at the end of the great tribulation.

What will be the outcome of this battle? John was given a preview: "And the beast was taken, and with him the false prophet . . . These both were cast alive into a lake of fire burning with brimstone" (v. 20). All their followers were slain (v. 21). This will end the short rule of the Antichrist over the earth.

MILLENNIUM

Six times in six consecutive verses (2-7) in chapter 20 we find the expression "thousand years." This is usually given its Latin designation, "millennium."

There are three different views held with regard to the millennium. *Premillennialism* holds that the second coming of Christ will occur before the millennium; *postmillennialism*, that it will take place after the millennium. *Amillennialism* is the view that there will be no literal millennium, no reign of Christ for a thousand years on earth. The expression here in Revelation 20 is taken as symbolical of the spiritual blessings of the believer's life in Christ. (The prefix *a* is the Greek negative. This view is sometimes called nil-millennialism.)

Today the majority of evangelicals are premillennialists.

But this was not always so. Most of the writers of the so-called "holiness classics" were postmillennialists, as was the early Nazarene theologian, A. M. Hills. When the writer attended college 40 years ago, the main teachers of both theology and philosophy were amillennialists. It is only in the present generation that premillennialism has become dominant among evangelicals.

The older postmillennialists expected an outpouring of the Holy Spirit at the end of this age that would bring in the kingdom of God. Today postmillennialism is generally discredited among evangelicals because in its newer forms it has usually been associated with a humanistic liberalism based on the belief in the natural improvement of society. But two world wars have now rather shattered the idea that mankind can bring in a millennium.

What is said about the millennium in chapter 20? We read first that Satan will be bound for the thousand years in "the bottomless pit" (Greek, *abyss*), so that he will not be able to "deceive the nations" (vv. 1-3). That has certainly not happened yet!

Then we are told that those who had been martyred for their loyalty to Christ will live and reign with Him for a thousand years (v. 4). "But the rest of the dead lived not again until the thousand years were finished. This is the first resurrection. Blessed and holy is he that hath part in the first resurrection: on such the second death hath no power, but they shall be priests of God and of Christ, and shall reign with him a thousand years" (vv. 5-6).

While only those who refused to obey the Antichrist are mentioned specifically in verse 4, the "they" who sat on thrones probably means Christ and His saints. It is commonly held that "the first resurrection" is the resurrection of all the righteous. This will take place before the millennium. The resurrection of the wicked will come after the millennium (v. 5).

At the end of the thousand years, "Satan shall be loosed

out of his prison [the bottomless pit], and shall go out to deceive the nations which are in the four quarters of the earth, Gog and Magog, to gather them together to battle" (vv. 7-8). This is what is commonly referred to as the Battle of Gog and Magog.

These two names have Old Testament reference. They occur together in Ezek. 38:2, and Gog is mentioned frequently in chapters 38 and 39. The ancient Jewish rabbis mentioned Gog and Magog as nations that will march against the Messiah. Many people in recent years have claimed that these two names represent Russia. The best scholarship today, however, does not accept this identification. It is true that current developments in the Middle East suggest that Russia may well become the main foe of Israel. But to affirm dogmatically that "Gog and Magog" means Russia is not sound exegesis. A careful reading of Rev. 20:8 will show that "Gog and Magog" is in direct apposition with "the nations which are in the four quarters of the earth"— in other words, all the nations that come against Christ and His followers.

One important point seems to be overlooked by those who identify Gog and Magog with Russia. They rightly point out the rapidly increasing influence of Russia in the Middle East. But the Battle of Gog and Magog is *after* the millennium. These names are not connected with the Battle of Armageddon *before* the millennium.

What will be the outcome of the Battle of Gog and Magog? Verse 9 tells us that the hosts of Satan "went up on the breadth of the earth, and compassed the camp of the saints about, and the beloved city: and fire came down from God out of heaven, and devoured them." Evidently the fighting will be extended to Jerusalem, and then a divine intervention will wipe out the enemy forces.

What is Satan's final fate? "And the devil that deceived them was cast into the lake of fire and brimstone, where the beast and the false prophet are, and shall be tormented day and night for ever and ever" (v. 10).

This event will be followed by the Judgment of the Great White Throne (vv. 11-13). Then we read: "And death and hell were cast into the lake of fire. This is the second death. And whosoever was not found written in the book of life was cast into the lake of fire" (vv. 14-15).

The word translated "hell" is *Hades*. Obviously "the lake of fire" is what we speak of as "hell." So it does not make sense to say that "death and hell delivered up the dead which were in them" (v. 13) or that "death and hell were cast into the lake of fire." *Hades* means the place of departed spirits, not the fire of eternal torment. The fact that this Greek word is translated "hell" 10 times in the King James Version (Matt. 11:23; 16:18; Luke 10:15; 16:23; Acts 2:27, 31; Rev. 1:18; 6:8; 20:13, 14) has created some confusion. On the other hand, *Gehenna*, which means a place of eternal, fiery torment, is correctly translated "hell" in all 12 places where it occurs.[7] It is death and the place of death that are cast into hell—"the lake of fire."

Hell is an awful fact to contemplate. We should be very sure that we are enrolled in the book of life, and should also do our best to bring others to an acceptance of Jesus Christ as their Saviour and Lord.

THE RAPTURE

This term is commonly used to designate the coming of Christ for His Church, or the rising of the saints "to meet the Lord in the air" (I Thess. 4:17). When will this take place?

Three answers are given to this question. The most popular view today is the *pre-tribulation* rapture; that is, Christ will come for His Church just before the great tribulation begins. So the saints will escape the awful sufferings of those days.

In recent years, an increasing number of evangelicals have expressed their belief in a *post-tribulation* rapture: the Church will be on earth during the great tribulation. In between these two is the view of a *mid-tribulation* rapture: just as the Israelites suffered in the first plagues on Egypt, so the Church will share in the sufferings of the early part of the tribulation period. This is really a modification of the pre-tribulation view, and it has been held by some very astute Bible expositors. It certainly has much to commend it. One advantage is that it escapes most of the strong objections leveled at both the other views.

Two factual observations need to be made. The first is that all three of these views are a part of premillennialism. Those who hold to a post-tribulation rapture are just as much premillennialists as those who hold to a pre-tribulation rapture. Both believe that Christ will come before the millennium. Pre-tribulationists differentiate between "the rapture"—Christ coming *for* His Church before the great tribulation—and "The Revelation"—Christ coming *with* His Church after the tribulation. They hold that the rapture is described in I Thess. 4:13-18 and I Cor. 15:52-54, and the Revelation in II Thessalonians 2. This explains the different points of view in the two Thessalonian passages. Post-tribulationists identify these as one event. They claim that the New Testament does not teach that there will be two phases to the Second Coming—the rapture before the great tribulation and the revelation after the tribulation—separated by three and a half years or by seven years, depending on whether one is a mid-tribulationist or a pre-tribulationist.[8]

The other factual observation is this: The teaching of a pre-tribulation rapture seems first to have been emphasized widely about 100 years ago by John Darby of the Plymouth Brethren. It was popularized in the United States by the Scofield Bible, which became *the* Bible of the Fundamentalists.

The well-informed Christian will recognize that each of these three views is held today by equally devout students of

77

the Word. And Christlike Christians will show respect for the adherents of all three.

A New Heaven and a New Earth

Chapters 21 and 22 mark a radical change from the main body of the Book of Revelation (cc. 6—20), where judgment and tribulation are an almost unbroken theme. Here we find the new, eternal order, and it is one of peace and righteousness.

John writes: "And I saw a new heaven and a new earth: for the first heaven and the first earth were passed away" (21:1; cf. 20:11). "*Heaven* here does not mean the eternal abode of God, but rather the astronomical space which man is now busy exploring with telescope and spacecraft."[9]

We are told that in this new earth there will be "no more sea." To the ancients, without compass or modern means of safety, the sea was a symbol of death (cf. 20:13). In the new heaven and new earth, death will be forever banned. Life will be eternal in God's presence.

The "new Jerusalem" (v. 2) has always been a favorite term among Christians. Many wax jubilant over the idea of walking through gates of pearl and on streets of gold (v. 21). But we should notice that this "city" is identified as "the bride, the Lamb's wife" (vv. 9-10). Obviously, then, all these materials that are mentioned are to be taken symbolically, in keeping with the nature of the Book of Revelation. What we have here is an attempt to describe the indescribable. Finite language is inadequate for portraying the infinite. John does his best to picture the superlative beauties of the next life. It should whet our eagerness for Christ to come and bring in the new order.

Twice in the twenty-second chapter we find the statement, "Behold, I come quickly" (vv. 7, 12). Because of this promise John is told: "Seal not the sayings of the prophecy of this book: for the time is at hand" (v. 10). This is in striking contrast to the command given to Daniel: "Shut up the words, and seal the book, even to the time of the end" (Dan. 12:4). Now, in the broadest sense, that time had come with the dawning of the Messianic age. So John is instructed not to seal his prophecies, but to give them openly. The words of verse 10 take on added significance in the light of present developments in the world.

Before "signing off," Jesus (v. 16) issues a beautiful invitation to all people to accept His salvation: "And the Spirit and the bride say, Come. And let him that heareth say, Come." Then—and there should always be a pause here—Jesus himself urges: "And let him that is athirst come. And whosoever will, let him take the water of life freely" (v. 17). As a part of "the bride," we should join with the Holy Spirit in saying, "Come," to all who need Christ. For the offer of eternal life is given to "whosoever will." Thus this capstone of divine revelation sounds a strong evangelistic note at the close. It is a reminder that we should not be so engrossed in the contemplation of heavenly beauties and blessings that we forget those around us who need salvation.

The last promise of the Bible is, "Surely I come quickly." The last prayer is (literally): "Amen! Come, Lord Jesus." Is that prayer ours today? Does His promise that He is coming soon fill our hearts with joy and anticipation? Or with dread and fear? If the latter, we should accept His gracious invitation to come to Him now, so that He may come to us then to receive us to himself. "Amen! Come, Lord Jesus."

79

11

This Generation

In the June 30, 1967, issue of *Time* the lead article in religion begins with this question: "Has the time now come for the erection of the third temple?"

The First Temple was built by Solomon about 966 B.C. and destroyed by the Babylonians in 586 B.C. The Second Temple was built by the returning captives in 516 B.C. Though rebuilt by Herod the Great shortly before the birth of Christ, it was still called the Second Temple, and it in turn was destroyed by the Romans in A.D. 70. Since then, for 1,900 years, the Jews have had no temple.

In the seventh century another tragedy overtook the Jews. The Moslems conquered Palestine, took Jerusalem, and converted the Temple site into a sacred Moslem area, still called Haram esh Sherif—the third most sacred Moslem spot, after Mecca and Medina. The Jews were excluded from their ancient Temple grounds.

The great medieval Jewish philosopher Maimonides said that every generation of Jews was responsible to rebuild the Temple *if* its site was ever retaken. It *was* retaken on June 7, 1967, on the third day of the Six-Day War. The story of what happened is as follows:

The Israeli Defense Forces rushed over Mount Zion and across no-man's-land south of the city, where no one had been allowed for 19 years (since 1948). They rounded the southeast corner of the Temple wall, which is also the outside city wall at that point, and started up the east side. When they reached what is sometimes called the Golden

Gate, they paused. This is the only gate in the eastern wall of the Temple area, and it has been blocked up with building stones for centuries.

Some of the soldiers wanted to break in here, thinking it would be the safest way to enter the city. But the commandant said: "No, we can't do that. Remember, the Messiah must be the first to enter this gate." (The Jews are still waiting, as they have for centuries, for the Messiah to come and open this gate.)

So the soldiers proceeded northward to St. Stephen's Gate, the only gateway in the eastern wall of the old city. There they finally broke through, after a bloody skirmish. Then they rushed down the main street until they reached an alley leading left to the Wailing Wall, which is part of the western wall of the Temple area. For centuries the Jews have prayed and wept there. But beginning with 1948 they were denied even this privilege, since all of the Old City had been designated as Arab territory.

When they reached the Wailing Wall, those tough Israeli soldiers fell on their knees in the cobblestone street and kissed the wall, weeping unashamedly. Then the senior chaplain of the Israeli forces, Rabbi Goren, raised his hand for silence and proclaimed: "We have taken the city of God. We are entering the Messianic era."

Today Jews are studying about Jesus as never before. One of the two fastest growing departments at the Hebrew University in Jerusalem in recent years has been the Department of Christian Studies. In four years (1964-67) 23 new books on Jesus were written by Jews in Hebrew and published in Israel, and every one was a sympathetic study of who Jesus of Nazareth really was.

In a paper he read at the Jerusalem Conference of Biblical Prophecy (June, 1971), Alex Wachtel told how he questioned some of his Jewish friends on their reaction to three positions: (1) Jesus was possessed by a devil; (2) Jesus was misguided; (3) Jesus was misunderstood. Practically all these Jews replied that they agreed with the third position.[1]

At the famous World Conference on Evangelism held in Berlin in 1966, there were several Jewish observers present from the United States. On the way back on the plane from Frankfurt to New York, one of them was sitting next to a Christian. He remarked that he was waiting for the coming of the Messiah.

The Christian said: "We also are looking for Him. But we believe it will be the return of Christ." And then he asked: "What would you do if you discovered when the Messiah does come that it was the same Jesus who visited Israel 2,000 years ago?"

With tears in his eyes the rabbi replied: "If it turned out to be Jesus, I would not be a bit surprised."[2]

In October, 1968, at the time of the Feast of Tabernacles, a prominent Jewish psychiatrist was speaking to a group of Arab and American Christians in Tel Aviv. Publicly he made the categorical statement: "Jesus of Nazareth is the Messiah of Israel."

Increase Mather graduated from Harvard at the age of 15 and later became its president. In 1669 he wrote: "When once God shall begin this work of Israel's salvation, it shall be carried on with speed and irresistible might. . . . All motions when they come near their center are most swift. The Israelites at their return shall even fly."

This brilliant Christian educator never dreamed how literally his prediction would be fulfilled. He used "fly" in a metaphorical sense. But 50,000 Jews were flown from Yemen to Israel and 100,000 from Iraq. This "Operation Flying Carpet" was completed in 1950 and 1951, when all Jews in these Arab countries were forced to leave.

Shortly after the close of the famous Six-Day War, as reported in the June 30, 1967, issue of *Time*, the Jewish historian Israel Eldad wrote: "We are at the stage where David was when he liberated Jerusalem." That was about 1000 B.C., when David took Jerusalem from the Jebusites and made it the capital of his new kingdom of Israel. Eldad continued: "From that time until the construction of the Temple by Solomon [about 966 B.C.] only one generation passed." And then he added this significant observation: "So it will be with us."

This gives new force to Jesus' words in Matt. 24:34— "Verily I say unto you, This generation shall not pass, till all these things be fulfilled."

Several interpretations have been offered for this verse. The most obvious application, of course, would be to A.D. 70, when the Romans destroyed the Temple at Jerusalem. This was in fulfillment of Jesus' prediction that this would happen, which He made in A.D. 30, just 40 years (one generation) before it happened.

But, as we have already noted in our study of the Olivet Discourse, the disciples not only asked, "When will this happen?" but, "What will be the sign of Your coming, and of the end of the age?" (Matt. 24:3, literal) In the Olivet Discourse, Jesus dealt with these larger questions. So His words in 24:34 cannot be limited to A.D. 70.

Another suggested interpretation is this: The word *genea* ("generation") also means "race." What Jesus meant was that the Jewish race would not pass away before His second coming.

Undeniably it is a miracle that the race of Israel still exists, after the terrible pogroms of the Middle Ages. A hundred years ago Bishop Lightfoot of the Church of England wrote: "You may deny if you will every successful miracle in the Bible, but this miracle—the preservation of Israel—is more convincing than all."

If those words were true a century ago, how much more true are they today! For in the years 1942-44 Adolf Hitler destroyed 6 million of the 9 million Jews in Europe. Not only that, but his purpose was to wipe out every last Jew on the face of the earth. In the July 12, 1968, issue of *Time*, Hitler is quoted as saying during the Second World War: "The end of the war will see the end of the Jewish race." Only divine intervention kept him from carrying out this diabolical intention.

But for years we have felt that these interpretations were not fully adequate. Was there a further meaning? We came to the conclusion that possibly these words could mean: The generation that saw the beginning of the fulfillment of these signs *might* see the end.

We turn back to Dan. 12:12, where we read: "Blessed is he that waiteth, and cometh to the thousand three hundred and five and thirty days." As already noted, Bible students commonly accept the "day=year" principle of prophecy. So this verse would suggest a lapse of 1,335 years.

Adam Clarke makes this comment: "If we reckon from A.D. 612, when Mohammedanism arose, they [the 1,335 years] lead us to 1947, when the fulness of the Gentiles shall be brought in." What happened in 1947? On November 21 of that year the United Nations passed a resolution in favor of the Jews having a national home in Palestine. The next year the new nation of Israel was set up. Now we ask: How could Adam Clarke, writing 150 years ago, predict to the very year the time when the Gentile domination of Palestine would come to an end? That domination began in 586 B.C., when the Babylonians destroyed Jerusalem. Except for a brief 80-year period of Maccabean Independence (143-63 B.C.), the Jews had no national status for 2,500 years. But 1947 changed it all, and since 1948 the Jews have had a strong and growing state of Israel.

But we turn back to Dan. 8:5—"And as I was considering, behold, an he goat came from the west on the face of the whole earth, and touched not the ground: and the goat had a notable horn between his eyes." Fortunately, we are not left in any doubt as to the matter of identification. Verse 21 reads: "And the rough goat is the king of Grecia: and the great horn that is between his eyes is the first king." That

85

would be Alexander the Great, the founder of the Greek Empire.

Alexander was not content to follow up the conquests made in Europe by his father, Philip of Macedon, but cast his eyes toward Asia. He dared to defy the invincible armies of the Persian Empire. Coming "from the west" (Europe), he hardly touched the ground as he defeated one army after another. He swept across Asia Minor and down through Syria and Palestine to Egypt. The main Egyptian seaport is still Alexandria, named after him.

We drop down to verse 8—"Therefore the he goat waxed very great." The Greek Empire spread over southeastern Europe, western Asia, and northeastern Africa, the first empire to bridge three continents. "And when he was strong"—when Alexander the Great was at the apex of his power—"the great horn was broken." Here is a vivid reference to the sudden, untimely death of Alexander in 323 B.C. at the early age of 32.

Now we turn to verse 14—"And he said unto me, Unto two thousand and three hundred days; and then shall the sanctuary be cleansed." We are aware, of course, that between verses 8 and 14 Daniel has been describing the persecution of the Jews by Antiochus Epiphanes in the second century B.C. But the end of verse 17 says: "Understand, O son of man: for at the time of the end shall be the vision." So this passage seems to refer not only primarily to Antiochus, but also finally to events "at the time of the end."

Adam Clarke says about the 2,300 years of verse 14: "If we date these years from the vision of the he-goat [Alexander's invasion of Asia] this was 334 B.C.; and 2,300 years from that time will reach to A.D. 1966"—when the sanctuary will be cleansed.

Perhaps the reader is saying, "Adam Clarke missed it by one year this time. The Jews regained Jerusalem and the Temple area in 1967." But he was not wrong. One would presume that from 1 B.C. to A.D. 1 would be two years. But actually 1 B.C. is A.U.C. (the year of Rome) 753, and A.D. 1 is A.U.C. 754. There is no zero year between B.C. and A.D. So we must add one year to the figure 1966, and we have 1967, when this took place.

Again we ask: How could Adam Clarke make these precise predictions 150 years ago exactly to the year, as we have now seen them fulfilled? We have no answer, unless this was what these scriptures were intended to mean.

We turn once again to chapter 12. In verse 4 Daniel is told to "shut up the words, and seal the book, even to the time of the end" (cf. v. 9). Apparently the meaning of his prophecies would not be understood until the end time. Now these prophecies are taking on fresh significance.

In the last part of verse 4 we have two interesting statements. The first is: "Many shall run to and fro." There never was a time before in human history when so many people were traveling so far as today. Our highways and skyways are filled with millions of people going somewhere. Even on multiple-lane highways, traffic sometimes comes to a standstill, the road being choked beyond capacity.

But people not only "go"; they "run." The standard rate of travel in the time of Christ was 15 to 20 miles per day. But one morning we boarded a plane in Sydney, Australia, at about nine in the morning. By that time in the evening we were on the ground at Tokyo, having flown about 6,600 miles, with stops at Manila and Hongkong. Yet, as a child, we went to church by horse and carriage. *In our own day* we have moved from the horse and wagon to jet travel. And we are not even discussing space flights.

Note now the second statement: "And knowledge shall increase." In the February, 1967, issue of the *Reader's Digest* an article asserted that the sum total of human knowledge doubled between 1775 and 1900—just 125 years. It doubled again between 1900 and 1950, only 50 years. It doubled again between 1950 and 1958, just eight years. The article went on to say that the sum total of human knowledge is thought to be doubling every five years!

How long did it take the population of the world to reach the billion mark? Many thousands of years, until 1830. How long did it take to get the second billion? Only a century, until 1931. How long for the third billion? Only 30 years, until 1961. Then the scientists were estimating that by the year 2000 there would be another 3 billion, but they have raised that estimate to 4 billion—an average of a billion every decade!

It hardly seems necessary to labor the point further. What we have already said amply proves that there has been more progress in scientific achievement in our generation than in all previous generations put together. We live in a new age—the jet age, the space age, the atomic age. We ought to be alert to this and keep constantly ready for our Lord's return.

Will Christ come in this generation? Only God knows the answer to that question. Jesus said that no man knows the day or the hour. But He warned us: "Watch therefore, for ye know not what hour your Lord doth come" (Matt. 24:42).

The songwriter expresses our feelings:

He's coming soon, He's coming soon;
With joy we welcome His returning.
It may be morn; it may be night or noon.
We know He's coming soon.

Reference Notes

INTRODUCTION

1. H. G. Liddell and Robert Scott, *A Greek-English Lexicon*, rev. H. S. Jones (Oxford: Clarendon Press, 1940), p. 1540.

2. *Ibid.*, p. 1539.

3. G. Abbott-Smith, *A Manual Greek Lexicon of the New Testament*, 2nd ed. (Edinburgh: T. & T. Clark, 1923), p. 390.

4. *Baker's Dictionary of Theology*, Everett F. Harrison, ed. (Grand Rapids, Mich.: Baker Book House, 1960), pp. 423-24.

CHAPTER 1

1. J. Paterson-Smyth, *A People's Life of Christ* (New York: Fleming H. Revell, 1920), p. 23.

2. *Ibid.*

3. *Ibid*, p. 26.

4. S. Angus, *Environment of Early Christianity* (New York: Charles Scribner's Sons, 1914), p. 222.

CHAPTER 2

1. W. F. Arndt and F. W. Gingrich, *A Greek-English Lexicon of the New Testament and Other Early Christian Literature* (Chicago: University of Chicago Press, 1957), p. 137.

CHAPTER 4

1. R. C. H. Lenski, *The Interpretation of the Acts of the Apostles* (Columbus, Ohio: Wartburg Press, 1944), p. 37.

CHAPTER 10

1. William Newell, *The Book of Revelation* (Chicago: Grace Publications, 1935), p. 5.

2. Edward McDowell, *The Meaning and Message of the Book of Revelation* (Nashville: Broadman Press, 1951), p. 24.

3. See the author's commentary on "Revelation" in *Beacon*

Bible Commentary (Kansas City: Beacon Hill Press of Kansas City, 1967), X, 577.

4. *Ibid.*, p. 578.

5. "Armageddon," *International Standard Bible Encyclopedia*, rev. ed. (Chicago: Howard Severance Co., 1929), II, 1340.

6. George E. Ladd, *A Commentary on the Revelation of John* (Grand Rapids, Mich.: Wm. B. Eerdmans Pub. Co., 1972), p. 216.

7. Seven times in Matthew, three times in Mark, once in Luke (12:5), and once in James (3:6).

8. For a post-tribulation view that puts strong emphasis on the imminent return of Christ, see J. Barton Payne, *The Imminent Appearing of Christ* (Grand Rapids, Mich.: Wm. B. Eerdmans Pub. Co., 1962).

9. BBC, X, 615.

Chapter 11

1. *Prophecy in the Making*, Carl F. H. Henry, ed. (Carol Stream, Ill.: Creation House, 1971), p. 157.

2. Arnold T. Olson, *Inside Jerusalem* (Glendale, Calif.: G/L Publications, 1968), p. 173.